THIS BOOK BELONGS TO

_____

START DATE

_____

EDITORIAL

EDITORS-IN-CHIEF
Raechel Myers & Amanda Bible Williams

CONTENT DIRECTOR
Russ Ramsey, MDiv., ThM.

MANAGING EDITOR
Jessica Lamb

EDITOR
Melanie Rainer

EDITORIAL ASSISTANT
Ellen Taylor

CREATIVE

CREATIVE DIRECTOR
Ryan Myers

ART DIRECTOR
Amanda Barnhart

DESIGNER
Kelsea Allen

SUPPORTING DESIGNER
Emily Knapp

ARTIST
Laci Fowler

PHOTOGRAPHERS
Rachel Moore, lifestyle
Amanda Barnhart, recipes

@SHEREADSTRUTH

SHEREADSTRUTH.COM

SUBSCRIPTION INQUIRIES
orders@shereadstruth.com

SHE READS TRUTH™

© 2018 by She Reads Truth, LLC

ISBN 978-1-946282-68-2

Though the dates in this book have been carefully researched, scholars disagree on the dating of many biblical events.

Biblical site locations are estimates based on archaeological evidence and biblical scholarship.

This book was printed offset in Nashville, Tennessee, on 70# Lynx Opaque. Cover is 100# Cougar Opaque with a soft touch lamination.

1 & 2

Corinthians

THE BODY OF CHRIST

SHE READS TRUTH

I work with a truly spectacular group of people, but we don't always see eye to eye.

Jessica, for example, is fiercely protective of words, watching over grammatical details like comma placement and hyphen length with laser-like focus. Ryan, I'm convinced, will defend the creative integrity of the She Reads Truth brand as long as he has breath, and Abby has yet to sit through a meeting without bringing to our attention the needs and desires of you, the Shes who read Truth with us. We all have different jobs, and sometimes it is our job to disagree.

Raechel and I learned this early on in working together, back when it was just the two of us: seeing things differently is a gift to be stewarded, not a tension to be avoided. Today there are eighteen of us at SRT headquarters, each bringing different skills and perspectives to the conference room table. But we are a team. We are here for each other, for the work set before us, and for you. Above all, we are here to hold out God's Word and bring glory to Him. Our differences help, not hinder, this pursuit.

It's easy for me to see God's provision in the differences among our team members. But I'm embarrassed to admit I often expect homogeneity in the Church. I find myself frustrated by our differences, bothered that we can't all agree on large and small aspects of our faith and life as followers of Jesus. I'm saddened when these differences go beyond disagreements to cause division and discouraged when these divisions are not easily overcome. I forget that God's Word and perfect wisdom are not diminished by our limited understanding or altered by our various opinions.

In his letters to the church at Corinth, the Apostle Paul encourages this congregation of young believers to embrace their common and primary identity in Christ. He desires for them to know and act on the truth that "we were all baptized by one Spirit into one body" and "we were all given one Spirit to drink" (1Co 12:13). The image of the Church as one body appears throughout these letters, making clear Paul's resounding declaration: we are many, but we are one in Christ.

Each map, chart, and theological extra in this study book is created to equip you to read and understand 1 & 2 Corinthians, both in their original context and application to our lives today. Take a close look at the Spiritual Gifts infographic and marvel at God's creativity among His people. Read the Lord's Supper chart and give thanks for the profound gift of salvation. Gather the women on your street or friends from your local church, enjoy the shareable recipes, and engage with the weekly study questions.

As you read 1 & 2 Corinthians, ask the Holy Spirit to open your eyes to see the Church all around you. Ask Him to teach you more about Himself, His body of believers, and the truth of His Word. Like the church at Corinth, we come to this text from a colorful array of backgrounds, experiences, and traditions. But we have a Savior who binds us. May His mercy and grace unite us as we read.

"The grace of the Lord Jesus Christ, and the love of God, and the fellowship of the Holy Spirit be with you all" (2Co 13:13).

Amanda

Amanda Bible Williams
EDITOR-IN-CHIEF

ALL RECIPES CONTAIN
5 INGREDIENTS OR LESS!

featured artists

PAINTINGS
LACI FOWLER

Laci is an artist focused on creating original artwork inspired by her life in Middle Tennessee, where she is renovating an historic home with her husband and son.

LIFESTYLE PHOTOGRAPHY
RACHEL MOORE

Rachel has been photographing weddings and families for ten years. She is drawn to the true, good, and beautiful and believes life is worth documenting. She resides in her hometown of Nashville with her musician husband and their son.

how to use this book

The Bible is living and active, breathed out by God, and we confidently hold it higher than anything we can do or say. Designed for a Monday start, this book focuses primarily on Scripture, with bonus resources to facilitate deeper engagement with God's Word.

SCRIPTURE READING

This study book presents 1 & 2 Corinthians in daily readings, plus supplemental passages for additional context.

Each weekday features space for personal reflection and prayer.

GRACE DAY

Use Saturdays to pray, rest, and reflect on what you've read.

WEEKLY TRUTH

Sundays are set aside for weekly Scripture memorization.

Find the corresponding memory cards in the back of this book.

STUDY QUESTIONS

Find weekly questions for personal or group reflection on pages 153–165.

For added community and conversation, join us in the **1 & 2 Corinthians** reading plan on the She Reads Truth app or at SheReadsTruth.com.

NATURAL BRUSH WRITING

BOLD FLORAL PAINTINGS

VIBRANT GREEN FOR GROWTH

EVERYDAY LIFESTYLE PHOTOGRAPHY

Design
ON PURPOSE

Paul's letter reminds us that the Church is one body made up of many parts. We were excited to express this concept through the color, design, and layout of this book.

The featured artwork, by artist Laci Fowler, was selected to serve as a visual interpretation of unity in diversity. Laci's landscapes and florals are comprised of loose, organic shapes in bold, textured brush strokes— different shapes working together to make a cohesive picture. Created using mixed mediums like acrylics, oil pastels, and gouache, these art pieces represent many believers coming together as one.

Our punchy green and chartreuse yellow color palette was inspired by the color and energy of the artwork. For lettering, we used a thick brush marker because it felt natural and quick, like a style used to jot down a short note.

Each recipe shared in this book has five or fewer ingredients with simple instructions for creating a final product that is, in whole, greater than its parts. At our recipe photo shoot, we had fun scattering the ingredients in a less-than-perfect style to emphasize how Christian community can be beautiful, even with its imperfections.

We hope these details draw you deeply into the inherently beautiful Word of God, and remind you of your own unique value in the body of Christ.

THE SHE READS TRUTH CREATIVE TEAM

first

1 CORINTHIANS

Key Verse

GOD IS FAITHFUL; YOU WERE CALLED BY
HIM INTO FELLOWSHIP WITH HIS SON,
JESUS CHRIST OUR LORD.

1 CORINTHIANS 1:9

ON THE TIMELINE:

Paul wrote his first letter to the Corinthian church during the last year of his three-year ministry at Ephesus, probably a few weeks before Pentecost in the spring of AD 56 (Ac 20:31; 1Co 15:32; 16:8).

A LITTLE BACKGROUND:

First Corinthians is the second letter Paul wrote to the Corinthian church. His earlier letter to Corinth, which was not included in the canon of Scripture but is referenced in 1 Corinthians 5:9, warned them not to associate with the sexually immoral. The writing of this second letter, 1 Corinthians, was prompted by reports of rivalry within the church (1:11). Paul addressed this in his letter, along with other troubling issues, including an incestuous relationship among the membership (5:1), division that arose during observance of the Lord's Supper (11:18), and confusion over the resurrection of the dead (15:12). As he was writing this letter to the Corinthian church, he must have received a letter from them asking his opinion on various issues because he included replies to those concerns as well (7:1, 25; 8:1; 12:1; 16:1).

MESSAGE & PURPOSE:

First Corinthians is the most literary of Paul's letters, using stylistic devices like irony, repetition, alliteration, and other wordplay to communicate the necessity of accepting the Lord's authority. Jesus is Lord and believers are His possession: this is the main theme of Paul's letter. For Paul, whatever issue was discussed, the answer always included a reminder of the Lord's authority over the Church (1:2, 10).

In addition to motivating the Corinthian church to acknowledge the Lord's ownership, Paul addressed key topics such as Christian unity, morality, the role of women, spiritual gifts, love, and the resurrection.

GIVE THANKS FOR THE
BOOK OF 1 CORINTHIANS:

First Corinthians contributes greatly to our understanding of Christian life, ministry, and relationships by showing us how the members of the Church—Christ's body—are to function together. Paul gave specific solutions to specific problems, but the underlying answer to them all is for the Church and its members to live Christ-centered lives.

BC

1000   900   800   700   600   500

Corinth in World History

TIMELINE

CORINTHIAN EVENTS

WORLD EVENTS

1000 BC

1 CITY OF CORINTH FOUNDED

900 BC

2 FIRST GOVERNMENT-ISSUED COIN CREATED BY CHINA

600 BC

3 LIGHTHOUSE INVENTED IN EGYPT

580 BC

4 PANHELLENIC ATHLETIC GAMES HELD IN CORINTH

550 BC

5 TEMPLE OF APOLLO CONSTRUCTED IN CORINTH

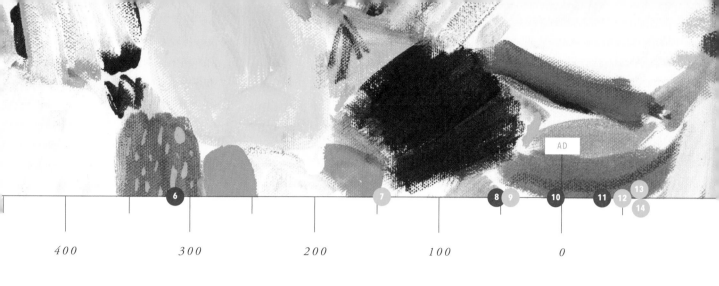

400   *300*   *200*   *100*   *0*

323 BC

6 DEATH OF ALEXANDER THE GREAT IN BABYLON

146 BC

7 CORINTH DESTROYED BY ROME

51 BC

8 CLEOPATRA NAMED CORULER OF EGYPT

44 BC

9 JULIUS CAESAR REBUILDS CORINTH AS A COLONY OF ROME

5 BC

10 BIRTH OF JESUS

AD *33*

11 DEATH, RESURRECTION, AND ASCENSION OF JESUS

AD *50-51*

12 CLAUDIUS ORDERS ALL JEWS TO LEAVE ROME

PAUL SPENDS 18 MONTHS IN CORINTH PLANTING A CHURCH

PAUL'S HEARING BEFORE CORINTH'S PROCONSUL, GALLIO

AD *56*

13 PAUL WRITES 1 & 2 CORINTHIANS

AD *57*

14 PAUL SPENDS A FEW MONTHS IN CORINTH WRITING ROMANS

Though the dates in this timeline have been carefully researched, scholars disagree on the precise year of Jesus' birth and the duration of His ministry prior to His crucifixion.

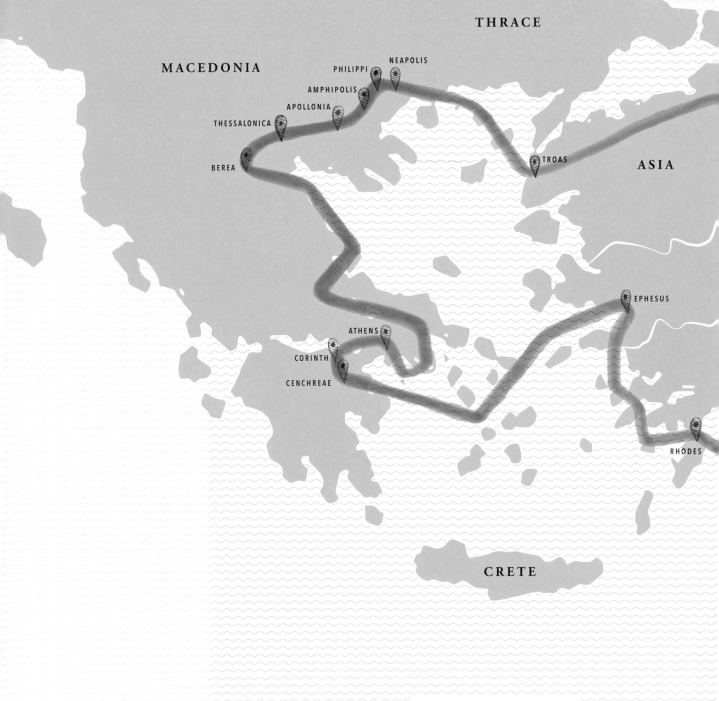

THRACE

MACEDONIA

NEAPOLIS

PHILIPPI

AMPHIPOLIS

APOLLONIA

THESSALONICA

BEREA

TROAS

ASIA

EPHESUS

ATHENS

CORINTH

CENCHREAE

RHODES

CRETE

MEDITERRANEAN SEA

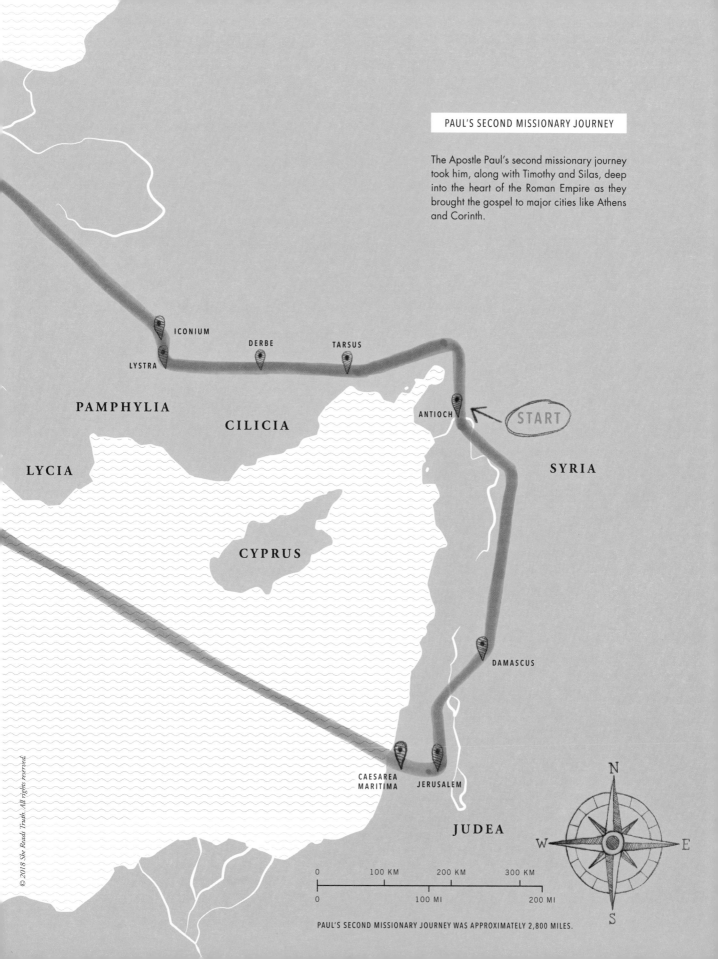

PAUL'S SECOND MISSIONARY JOURNEY

The Apostle Paul's second missionary journey took him, along with Timothy and Silas, deep into the heart of the Roman Empire as they brought the gospel to major cities like Athens and Corinth.

ICONIUM

DERBE

TARSUS

LYSTRA

PAMPHYLIA

CILICIA

ANTIOCH

START

LYCIA

SYRIA

CYPRUS

DAMASCUS

CAESAREA
MARITIMA

JERUSALEM

JUDEA

N

W   E

S

0   100 KM   200 KM   300 KM

0   100 MI   200 MI

PAUL'S SECOND MISSIONARY JOURNEY WAS APPROXIMATELY 2,800 MILES.

Week One

DAY 1

*Christ the Power and
Wisdom of God*

1 CORINTHIANS 1
GREETING

¹ Paul, called as an apostle of Christ Jesus by God's will, and Sosthenes our brother:

² To the church of God at Corinth, to those sanctified in Christ Jesus, called as saints, with all those in every place who call on the name of Jesus Christ our Lord—both their Lord and ours.

³ Grace to you and peace from God our Father and the Lord Jesus Christ.

THANKSGIVING

⁴ I always thank my God for you because of the grace of God given to you in Christ Jesus, ⁵ that you were enriched in him in every way, in all speech and all knowledge. ⁶ In this way, the testimony about Christ was confirmed among you, ⁷ so that you do not lack any spiritual gift as you eagerly wait for the revelation of our Lord Jesus Christ. ⁸ He will also strengthen you to the end, so that you will be blameless in the day of our Lord Jesus

"Celebrate," Mixed media on canvas, 16x20

Christ. ⁹ God is faithful; you were called by him into fellowship with his Son, Jesus Christ our Lord.

DIVISIONS AT CORINTH

¹⁰ Now I urge you, brothers and sisters, in the name of our Lord Jesus Christ, that all of you agree in what you say, that there be no divisions among you, and that you be united with the same understanding and the same conviction. ¹¹ For it has been reported to me about you, my brothers and sisters, by members of Chloe's people, that there is rivalry among you. ¹² What I am saying is this: One of you says, "I belong to Paul," or "I belong to Apollos," or "I belong to Cephas," or "I belong to Christ." ¹³ Is Christ divided? Was Paul crucified for you? Or were you baptized in Paul's name? ¹⁴ I thank God that I baptized none of you except Crispus and Gaius, ¹⁵ so that no one can say you were baptized in my name. ¹⁶ I did, in fact, baptize the household of Stephanas; beyond that, I don't recall if I baptized anyone else. ¹⁷ For Christ did not send me to baptize, but to preach the gospel—not with eloquent wisdom, so that the cross of Christ will not be emptied of its effect.

CHRIST THE POWER AND WISDOM OF GOD

STUDY QUESTIONS ON P. 154

¹⁸ For the word of the cross is foolishness to those who are perishing, but it is the power of God to us who are being saved.

¹⁹ For it is written,

> I will destroy the wisdom of the wise,
> and I will set aside the intelligence of the intelligent.

²⁰ Where is the one who is wise? Where is the teacher of the law? Where is the debater of this age? Hasn't God made the world's wisdom foolish? ²¹ For since, in God's wisdom, the world did not know God through wisdom, God was pleased to save those who believe through the foolishness of what is preached. ²² For the Jews ask for signs and the Greeks seek wisdom, ²³ but we preach Christ crucified, a stumbling block to the Jews and foolishness to the Gentiles. ²⁴ Yet to those who are called, both Jews and Greeks, Christ is the power of God and the wisdom of God, ²⁵ because God's foolishness is wiser than human wisdom, and God's weakness is stronger than human strength.

BOASTING ONLY IN THE LORD

²⁶ Brothers and sisters, consider your calling: Not many were wise from a human perspective, not many powerful, not many of noble birth. ²⁷ Instead, God has chosen what is foolish in the world to shame the wise, and God has chosen what

is weak in the world to shame the strong. [28] God has chosen what is insignificant and despised in the world—what is viewed as nothing—to bring to nothing what is viewed as something, [29] so that no one may boast in his presence. [30] It is from him that you are in Christ Jesus, who became wisdom from God for us—our righteousness, sanctification, and redemption, [31] in order that, as it is written: Let the one who boasts, boast in the Lord.

EXODUS 19:5-6

[5] "'Now if you will carefully listen to me and keep my covenant, you will be my own possession out of all the peoples, although the whole earth is mine, [6] and you will be my kingdom of priests and my holy nation.' These are the words that you are to say to the Israelites."

JAMES 1:18

By his own choice, he gave us birth by the word of truth so that we would be a kind of firstfruits of his creatures.

DAY 2

Spiritual Wisdom

1 CORINTHIANS 2
PAUL'S PROCLAMATION

¹ When I came to you, brothers and sisters, announcing the mystery of God to you, I did not come with brilliance of speech or wisdom. ² I decided to know nothing among you except Jesus Christ and him crucified. ³ I came to you in weakness, in fear, and in much trembling. ⁴ My speech and my preaching were not with persuasive words of wisdom but with a demonstration of the Spirit's power, ⁵ so that your faith might not be based on human wisdom but on God's power.

SPIRITUAL WISDOM

⁶ We do, however, speak a wisdom among the mature, but not a wisdom of this age, or of the rulers of this age, who are coming to nothing. ⁷ On the contrary, we speak God's hidden wisdom in a mystery, a wisdom God predestined before the ages for our glory. ⁸ None of the rulers of this age knew this wisdom, because if they had known it, they would not have crucified the Lord of glory. ⁹ But as it is written,

What no eye has seen, no ear has heard,
and no human heart has conceived—
God has prepared these things for those who
love him.

¹⁰ Now God has revealed these things to us by the Spirit, since the Spirit searches everything, even the depths of God. ¹¹ For who knows a person's thoughts except his spirit within him? In the same way, no one knows the thoughts of God except the Spirit of God. ¹² Now we have not received the spirit of the world, but the Spirit who comes from God, so that we may understand what has been freely given to us by God. ¹³ We also speak these things, not in words taught by human wisdom, but in those taught by the Spirit, explaining spiritual things to spiritual people. ¹⁴ But the person without the Spirit does not receive what comes from God's Spirit, because it is foolishness to him; he is not able to understand it since it is evaluated spiritually. ¹⁵ The spiritual person,

however, can evaluate everything, and yet he himself cannot be evaluated by anyone. ¹⁶ For

who has known the Lord's mind,
that he may instruct him?

But we have the mind of Christ.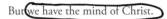

ROMANS 8:26-30

²⁶ In the same way the Spirit also helps us in our weakness, because we do not know what to pray for as we should, but the Spirit himself intercedes for us with unspoken groanings. ²⁷ And he who searches our hearts knows the mind of the Spirit, because he intercedes for the saints according to the will of God.

²⁸ We know that all things work together for the good of those who love God, who are called according to his purpose.

²⁹ For those he foreknew he also predestined to be conformed to the image of his Son, so that he would be the firstborn among many brothers and sisters. ³⁰ And those he predestined, he also called; and those he called, he also justified; and those he justified, he also glorified.

EPHESIANS 1:13-14

¹³ In him you also were sealed with the promised Holy Spirit when you heard the word of truth, the gospel of your salvation, and when you believed. ¹⁴ The Holy Spirit is the down payment of our inheritance, until the redemption of the possession, to the praise of his glory.

God
the
Spirit

WHAT IS THE HOLY SPIRIT?

AN EXCERPT FROM
*THE BOOK OF COMMON
PRAYER* CATECHISM

The Holy Spirit is the third person of the Trinity, God at work in the world and in the Church even now.

JB 32:8; MT 28:19; LK 3:22;
JN 14:25-26; 1JN 5:6-8

HOW IS THE HOLY SPIRIT REVEALED IN THE OLD COVENANT?

A catechism is a series of questions and answers used to teach foundational doctrines of faith.

The Holy Spirit is revealed in the old covenant as the giver of life; the One who spoke through the prophets.

GN 1:1-2; JB 33:4; PS 104:30;
IS 61:1-3; EZK 2:2; 11:5; JL 2:28

HOW IS THE HOLY SPIRIT REVEALED IN THE NEW COVENANT?

The Holy Spirit is revealed as the Lord who leads us into all truth and enables us to grow in the likeness of Christ.

JN 16:13; AC 1:4-8; 2:16-21;
1CO 2:10-13; 2CO 3:18; 1PT 1:1-2

HOW DO WE RECOGNIZE THE PRESENCE OF THE HOLY SPIRIT IN OUR LIVES?

We recognize the presence of the Holy Spirit when we confess Jesus Christ as Lord and are brought into love and harmony with God, with ourselves, with our neighbors, and with all creation.

PS 139:7; RM 8:1-11; 10:9,
EPH 1:13-14; TI 3:6-7; 1JN 4:13-15

HOW DO WE RECOGNIZE THE TRUTHS TAUGHT BY THE HOLY SPIRIT?

We recognize truths to be taught by the Holy Spirit when they are in accord with the Scriptures.

NEH 9:20; PS 143:10; JN 15:26;
2CO 2:10-16; 1TH 1:5; 2TM 3:16-17

DAY 3

The Role of God's Servants

1 CORINTHIANS 3

THE PROBLEM OF IMMATURITY

¹ For my part, brothers and sisters, I was not able to speak to you as spiritual people but as people of the flesh, as babies in Christ. ² I gave you milk to drink, not solid food, since you were not yet ready for it. In fact, you are still not ready, ³ because you are still worldly. For since there is envy and strife among you, are you not worldly and behaving like mere humans? ⁴ For whenever someone says, "I belong to Paul," and another, "I belong to Apollos," are you not acting like mere humans?

THE ROLE OF GOD'S SERVANTS

⁵ What then is Apollos? What is Paul? They are servants through whom you believed, and each has the role the Lord has given. ⁶ I planted, Apollos watered, but God gave the growth. ⁷ So then neither the one who plants nor the one who waters is anything, but only God who gives the growth. ⁸ Now he who plants and he who waters are one, and each will receive his own reward according to his own labor. ⁹ For we are God's coworkers. You are God's field, God's building.

¹⁰ According to God's grace that was given to me, I have laid a foundation as a skilled master builder, and another builds on it. But each one is to be careful how he builds on it. ¹¹ For no one can lay any other foundation than what has been laid down. That foundation is Jesus Christ. ¹² If anyone builds on the foundation with gold, silver, costly stones, wood, hay, or straw, ¹³ each one's work will become obvious. For the day will disclose it, because it will be revealed by fire; the fire will test the quality of each one's work. ¹⁴ If anyone's work that he has built survives, he will receive a reward. ¹⁵ If anyone's work is burned up, he will experience loss, but he himself will be saved—but only as through fire.

¹⁶ Don't you yourselves know that you are God's temple and that the Spirit of God lives in you? ¹⁷ If anyone destroys God's temple, God will destroy him; for God's temple is holy, and that is what you are.

THE FOLLY OF HUMAN WISDOM

[18] Let no one deceive himself. If anyone among you thinks he is wise in this age, let him become a fool so that he can become wise. [19] For the wisdom of this world is foolishness with God, since it is written, He catches the wise in their craftiness; [20] and again, The Lord knows that the reasonings of the wise are futile. [21] So let no one boast in human leaders, for everything is yours— [22] whether Paul or Apollos or Cephas or the world or life or death or things present or things to come—

everything is yours, [23] and you belong to Christ, and Christ belongs to God.

JOHN 5:24

"Truly I tell you, anyone who hears my word and believes him who sent me has eternal life and will not come under judgment but has passed from death to life."

ROMANS 5:1

Therefore, since we have been declared righteous by faith, we have peace with God through our Lord Jesus Christ.

6-8-18

DAY 4

The Faithful Manager

1 CORINTHIANS 4
THE FAITHFUL MANAGER

[1] A person should think of us in this way: as servants of Christ and managers of the mysteries of God. [2] In this regard, it is required that managers be found faithful. [3] It is of little importance to me that I should be judged by you or by any human court. In fact, I don't even judge myself. [4] For I am not conscious of anything against myself, but I am not justified by this. It is the Lord who judges me. [5] So don't judge anything prematurely, before the Lord comes, who will both bring to light what is hidden in darkness and reveal the intentions of the hearts. And then praise will come to each one from God.

THE APOSTLES' EXAMPLE OF HUMILITY

[6] Now, brothers and sisters, I have applied these things to myself and Apollos for your benefit, so that you may learn from us the meaning of the saying: "Nothing beyond what is written." The purpose is that none of you will be arrogant, favoring one person over another. [7] For who makes you so superior? What do you have that you didn't receive? If, in fact, you did receive it, why do you boast as if you hadn't received it? [8] You are already full! You are already rich! You have begun to reign as kings without us—and I wish you did reign, so that we could also reign with you! [9] For I think God has displayed us, the apostles, in last place, like men condemned to die: We have become a spectacle to the world, both to angels and to people. [10] We are fools for Christ, but you are wise in Christ! We are weak, but you are strong! You are distinguished, but we are dishonored! [11] Up to the present hour we are both hungry and thirsty; we are poorly clothed, roughly treated, homeless; [12] we labor, working with our own hands. When we are reviled, we bless; when we are persecuted, we endure it; [13] when we are slandered, we respond graciously. Even now, we are like the scum of the earth, like everyone's garbage.

PAUL'S FATHERLY CARE

[14] I'm not writing this to shame you, but to warn you as my dear children. [15] For you may have

countless instructors in Christ, but you don't have many fathers. For I became your father in Christ Jesus through the gospel. [16] Therefore I urge you to imitate me. [17] This is why I have sent Timothy to you. He is my dearly loved and faithful child in the Lord. He will remind you about my ways in Christ Jesus, just as I teach everywhere in every church.

[18] Now some are arrogant, as though I were not coming to you. [19] But I will come to you soon, if the Lord wills, and I will find out not the talk, but the power of those who are arrogant. [20] For the kingdom of God is not a matter of talk but of power. [21] What do you want? Should I come to you with a rod, or in love and a spirit of gentleness?

ZEPHANIAH 2:3

Seek the LORD, all you humble of the earth,
who carry out what he commands.

Seek righteousness, seek humility;

perhaps you will be concealed
on the day of the LORD's anger.

1 PETER 5:5

In the same way, you who are younger, be subject to the elders. All of you clothe yourselves with humility toward one another, because

God resists the proud
but gives grace to the humble.

6-11-18

DAY 5

Church Discipline

1 CORINTHIANS 5
IMMORAL CHURCH MEMBERS

[1] It is actually reported that there is sexual immorality among you, and the kind of sexual immorality that is not even tolerated among the Gentiles—a man is sleeping with his father's wife. [2] And you are arrogant! Shouldn't you be filled with grief and remove from your congregation the one who did this? [3] Even though I am absent in the body, I am present in spirit. As one who is present with you in this way, I have already pronounced judgment on the one who has been doing such a thing. [4] When you are assembled in the name of our Lord Jesus, and I am with you in spirit, with the power of our Lord Jesus, [5] hand that one over to Satan for the destruction of the flesh, so that his spirit may be saved in the day of the Lord.

[6] Your boasting is not good.

Don't you know that a little leaven leavens the whole batch of dough?

[7] Clean out the old leaven so that you may be a new unleavened batch, as indeed you are. For Christ our Passover lamb has been sacrificed. [8] Therefore, let us observe the feast, not with old leaven or with the leaven of malice and evil, but with the unleavened bread of sincerity and truth.

CHURCH DISCIPLINE

[9] I wrote to you in a letter not to associate with sexually immoral people. [10] I did not mean the immoral people of this world or the greedy and swindlers or idolaters; otherwise you would have to leave the world. [11] But actually, I wrote you not to associate with anyone who claims to be a brother or sister and is sexually immoral or greedy, an idolater or verbally abusive, a drunkard or a swindler. Do not even eat with such a person. [12] For what business is it of mine to judge outsiders? Don't you judge those who are inside? [13] God judges outsiders. Remove the evil person from among you.

LEVITICUS 18:8

You are not to have sex with your father's wife; she is your father's family.

GALATIANS 6:1-10

[1] Brothers and sisters, if someone is overtaken in any wrongdoing, you who are spiritual, restore such a person with a gentle spirit, watching out for yourselves so that you also won't be tempted. [2] Carry one another's burdens; in this way you will fulfill the law of Christ. [3] For if anyone considers himself to be something when he is nothing, he deceives himself. [4] Let each person examine his own work, and then he can take pride in himself alone, and not compare himself with someone else. [5] For each person will have to carry his own load.

[6] Let the one who is taught the word share all his good things with the teacher. [7] Don't be deceived: God is not mocked. For whatever a person sows he will also reap, [8] because the one who sows to his flesh will reap destruction from the flesh, but the one who sows to the Spirit will reap eternal life from the Spirit. [9] Let us not get tired of doing good, for we will reap at the proper time if we don't give up. [10] Therefore, as we have opportunity, let us work for the good of all, especially for those who belong to the household of faith.

Bacon-Wrapped Dates

INGREDIENTS: 3 | MAKES: 16 BITES

1

16 DATES

2

4 OUNCES
GOAT CHEESE

3

8 SLICES
THIN BACON, HALVED

EXTRA

TOOTHPICKS

DIRECTIONS

Preheat oven to 350°F.

Slice dates lengthwise on one side to create an opening and remove pits. Use a spoon to fill each opening with goat cheese. Press the sides together.

Wrap dates with bacon and secure with a toothpick. Arrange upright on a lined baking sheet with raised edges. Bake 10 minutes.

Turn each date on its side. Bake 5 to 8 minutes more until browned, then turn dates on the other side and repeat.

Transfer to a plate lined with paper towels. Let stand 5 minutes before serving.

GRACE DAY

Use this day to pray, rest, and reflect on this week's reading, giving thanks for the grace that is ours in Christ.

Therefore, since we have been declared righteous by faith, we have peace with God through our Lord Jesus Christ.

ROMANS 5:1

Scripture is God-breathed and true. When we memorize it, we carry the gospel with us wherever we go.

This week we will memorize the key verse for 1 Corinthians.

God is faithful; you were called by him into fellowship with his Son, Jesus Christ our Lord.

1 CORINTHIANS 1:9

Find the corresponding memory card in the back of this book.

Week Two

DAY 8

---

*Glorifying God in
Body and Spirit*

1 CORINTHIANS 6
LAWSUITS AMONG BELIEVERS

[1] If any of you has a dispute against another, how dare you take it to court before the unrighteous, and not before the saints? [2] Or don't you know that the saints will judge the world? And if the world is judged by you, are you unworthy to judge the trivial cases? [3] Don't you know that we will judge angels—how much more matters of this life? [4] So if you have such matters, do you appoint as your judges those who have no standing in the church? [5] I say this to your shame! Can it be that there is not one wise person among you who is able to arbitrate between fellow believers? [6] Instead, brother goes to court against brother, and that before unbelievers!

[7] As it is, to have legal disputes against one another is already a defeat for you. Why not rather be wronged? Why not rather be cheated? [8] Instead, you yourselves do wrong and cheat—and you do this to brothers and sisters! [9] Don't you know that the unrighteous will not inherit God's kingdom? Do not be deceived: No sexually immoral people, idolaters, adulterers, or males who have sex with

41

males, [10] no thieves, greedy people, drunkards, verbally abusive people, or swindlers will inherit God's kingdom. [11] And some of you used to be like this.

But you were washed, you were sanctified, you were justified in the name of the Lord Jesus Christ and by the Spirit of our God.

GLORIFYING GOD IN BODY AND SPIRIT

STUDY QUESTIONS ON P. 156

[12] "Everything is permissible for me," but not everything is beneficial. "Everything is permissible for me," but I will not be mastered by anything. [13] "Food is for the stomach and the stomach for food," and God will do away with both of them. However, the body is not for sexual immorality but for the Lord, and the Lord for the body. [14] God raised up the Lord and will also raise us up by his power. [15] Don't you know that your bodies are a part of Christ's body? So should I take a part of Christ's body and make it part of a prostitute? Absolutely not! [16] Don't you know that anyone joined to a prostitute is one body with her? For Scripture says, The two will become one flesh. [17] But anyone joined to the Lord is one spirit with him.

[18] Flee sexual immorality! Every other sin a person commits is outside the body, but the person who is sexually immoral sins against his own body. [19] Don't you know that your body is a temple of the Holy Spirit who is in you, whom you have from God? You are not your own, [20] for you were bought at a price. So glorify God with your body.

MATTHEW 18:15-20
RESTORING A BROTHER

[15] "If your brother sins against you, go and rebuke him in private. If he listens to you, you have won your brother. [16] But if he won't listen, take one or two others with you, so that by the testimony of two or three witnesses every fact may be established. [17] If he doesn't pay attention to them, tell the church. If he doesn't pay attention even to the church, let him be like a Gentile and a tax collector to you. [18] Truly I tell you, whatever you bind on earth will have been bound in heaven, and whatever you loose on earth will have been loosed in heaven. [19] Again, truly I tell you, if two of you on earth agree about any matter that you pray for, it will be done for you by my Father in heaven. [20] For where two or three are gathered together in my name, I am there among them."

TITUS 3:4-7

[4] But when the kindness of God our Savior and his love for mankind appeared, [5] he saved us—not by works of righteousness that we had done, but according to his mercy—through the washing of regeneration and renewal by the Holy Spirit. [6] He poured out his Spirit on us abundantly through Jesus Christ our Savior [7] so that, having been justified by his grace, we may become heirs with the hope of eternal life.

DAY 9

Principles of Marriage

1 CORINTHIANS 7

PRINCIPLES OF MARRIAGE

¹ Now in response to the matters you wrote about: "It is good for a man not to use a woman for sex." ² But because sexual immorality is so common, each man should have sexual relations with his own wife, and each woman should have sexual relations with her own husband. ³ A husband should fulfill his marital duty to his wife, and likewise a wife to her husband. ⁴ A wife does not have the right over her own body, but her husband does. In the same way, a husband does not have the right over his own body, but his wife does. ⁵ Do not deprive one another—except when you agree for a time, to devote yourselves to prayer. Then come together again; otherwise, Satan may tempt you because of your lack of self-control. ⁶ I say this as a concession, not as a command. ⁷ I wish that all people were as I am. But each has his own gift from God, one person has this gift, another has that.

A WORD TO THE UNMARRIED

⁸ I say to the unmarried and to widows: It is good for them if they remain as I am. ⁹ But if they do not have self-control, they should marry, since it is better to marry than to burn with desire.

ABOUT MARRIED PEOPLE

¹⁰ To the married I give this command—not I, but the Lord—a wife is not to leave her husband. ¹¹ But if she does leave, she must remain unmarried or be reconciled to her husband—and a husband is not to divorce his wife. ¹² But I (not the Lord) say to the rest: If any brother has an unbelieving wife and she is willing to live with him, he must not divorce her. ¹³ Also, if any woman has an unbelieving husband and he is willing to live with her, she must not divorce her husband. ¹⁴ For the unbelieving husband is made holy by the wife, and the unbelieving wife is made holy by the husband. Otherwise your children would

CONTINUED

GOD HAS CALLED YOU TO LIVE IN PEACE.

1 CORINTHIANS 7:15

be unclean, but as it is they are holy. [15] But if the unbeliever leaves, let him leave. A brother or a sister is not bound in such cases. God has called you to live in peace. [16] Wife, for all you know, you might save your husband. Husband, for all you know, you might save your wife.

VARIOUS SITUATIONS OF LIFE

[17] Let each one live his life in the situation the Lord assigned when God called him. This is what I command in all the churches. [18] Was anyone already circumcised when he was called? He should not undo his circumcision. Was anyone called while uncircumcised? He should not get circumcised. [19] Circumcision does not matter and uncircumcision does not matter. Keeping God's commands is what matters. [20] Let each of you remain in the situation in which he was called. [21] Were you called while a slave? Don't let it concern you. But if you can become free, by all means take the opportunity. [22] For he who is called by the Lord as a slave is the Lord's freedman. Likewise he who is called as a free man is Christ's slave. [23] You were bought at a price; do not become slaves of people. [24] Brothers and sisters, each person is to remain with God in the situation in which he was called.

ABOUT THE UNMARRIED AND WIDOWS

[25] Now about virgins: I have no command from the Lord, but I do give an opinion as one who by the Lord's mercy is faithful. [26] Because of the present distress, I think that it is good for a man to remain as he is. [27] Are you bound to a wife? Do not seek to be released. Are you released from a wife? Do not seek a wife. [28] However, if you do get married, you have not sinned, and if a virgin marries, she has not sinned. But such people will have trouble in this life, and I am trying to spare you.

[29] This is what I mean, brothers and sisters: The time is limited, so from now on those who have wives should be as though they had none, [30] those who weep as though they did not weep, those who rejoice as though they did not rejoice, those who buy as though they didn't own anything, [31] and those who use the world as though they did not make full use of it.

For this world in its current form is passing away.

[32] I want you to be without concerns. The unmarried man is concerned about the things of the Lord—how he may please the Lord. [33] But the married man is concerned about the things of the world—how he may please his wife— [34] and his interests are divided. The unmarried woman or virgin is concerned about the things of the Lord, so that she may be holy both in body and in spirit. But the married woman is concerned about the things of the world—how she may please her husband. [35] I am saying this for your own benefit, not to put a restraint on

you, but to promote what is proper and so that you may be devoted to the Lord without distraction.

[36] If any man thinks he is acting improperly toward the virgin he is engaged to, if she is getting beyond the usual age for marriage, and he feels he should marry—he can do what he wants. He is not sinning; they can get married. [37] But he who stands firm in his heart (who is under no compulsion, but has control over his own will) and has decided in his heart to keep her as his fiancé, will do well. [38] So then he who marries his fiancé does well, but he who does not marry will do better.

[39] A wife is bound as long as her husband is living. But if her husband dies, she is free to be married to anyone she wants—only in the Lord. [40] But she is happier if she remains as she is, in my opinion. And I think that I also have the Spirit of God.

GENESIS 2:24

This is why a man leaves his father and mother and bonds with his wife, and they become one flesh.

DAY 10

Food Offered to Idols

1 CORINTHIANS 8
FOOD OFFERED TO IDOLS

¹ Now about food sacrificed to idols: We know that "we all have knowledge." Knowledge puffs up, but love builds up. ² If anyone thinks he knows anything, he does not yet know it as he ought to know it. ³ But if anyone loves God, he is known by him.

⁴ About eating food sacrificed to idols, then, we know that "an idol is nothing in the world," and that "there is no God but one." ⁵ For even if there are so-called gods, whether in heaven or on earth—as there are many "gods" and many "lords"— ⁶ yet for us there is one God, the Father. All things are from him, and we exist for him. And there is one Lord, Jesus Christ. All things are through him, and we exist through him.

⁷ However, not everyone has this knowledge. Some have been so used to idolatry up until now that when they eat food sacrificed to an idol, their conscience, being weak, is defiled. ⁸ Food will not bring us close to God. We are not worse off if we don't eat, and we are not better if we do eat. ⁹ But be careful that this right of yours in no way becomes a stumbling block to the weak. ¹⁰ For if someone sees you, the one who has knowledge, dining in an idol's temple, won't his weak conscience be encouraged to eat food offered to idols? ¹¹ So the weak person, the brother or sister for whom Christ died, is ruined by your knowledge. ¹² Now when you sin like this against brothers and sisters and wound their weak conscience, you are sinning against Christ. ¹³ Therefore, if food causes my brother or sister to fall, I will never again eat meat,

so that I won't cause my brother or sister to fall.

JOHN 10:14-16
¹⁴ "I am the good shepherd. I know my own, and my own know me, ¹⁵ just as the Father knows me, and I know the Father. I lay down my life for the

sheep. [16] But I have other sheep that are not from this sheep pen; I must bring them also, and they will listen to my voice. Then there will be one flock, one shepherd."

2 TIMOTHY 2:14-19

[14] Remind them of these things, and charge them before God not to fight about words. This is useless and leads to the ruin of those who listen. [15] Be diligent to present yourself to God as one approved, a worker who doesn't need to be ashamed, correctly teaching the word of truth. [16] Avoid irreverent and empty speech, since those who engage in it will produce even more godlessness, [17] and their teaching will spread like gangrene. Hymenaeus and Philetus are among them. [18] They have departed from the truth, saying that the resurrection has already taken place, and are ruining the faith of some. [19] Nevertheless, God's solid foundation stands firm, bearing this inscription: The Lord knows those who are his, and let everyone who calls on the name of the Lord turn away from wickedness.

DAY 11

Paul's Example

1 CORINTHIANS 9
PAUL'S EXAMPLE AS AN APOSTLE

¹ Am I not free? Am I not an apostle? Have I not seen Jesus our Lord? Are you not my work in the Lord? ² If I am not an apostle to others, at least I am to you, because you are the seal of my apostleship in the Lord.

³ My defense to those who examine me is this: ⁴ Don't we have the right to eat and drink? ⁵ Don't we have the right to be accompanied by a believing wife like the other apostles, the Lord's brothers, and Cephas? ⁶ Or do only Barnabas and I have no right to refrain from working? ⁷ Who serves as a soldier at his own expense? Who plants a vineyard and does not eat its fruit? Or who shepherds a flock and does not drink the milk from the flock?

⁸ Am I saying this from a human perspective? Doesn't the law also say the same thing? ⁹ For it is written in the law of Moses, Do not muzzle an ox while it treads out grain. Is God really concerned about oxen? ¹⁰ Isn't he really saying it for our sake? Yes, this is written for our sake, because

> *he who plows ought to plow in hope, and he who threshes should thresh in hope of sharing the crop.*

¹¹ If we have sown spiritual things for you, is it too much if we reap material benefits from you? ¹² If others have this right to receive benefits from you, don't we even more? Nevertheless, we have not made use of this right; instead, we endure everything so that we will not hinder the gospel of Christ.

¹³ Don't you know that those who perform the temple services eat the food from the temple, and those who serve at the altar share in the offerings of the altar? ¹⁴ In the same way, the Lord has commanded that those who preach the gospel should earn their living by the gospel.

¹⁵ For my part I have used none of these rights, nor have I written these things that they may be applied in my case. For it would be better for me to die than for anyone to deprive me of my boast! ¹⁶ For if I preach the gospel, I have no reason to boast, because I am compelled to preach—and woe to me if I do not preach the gospel! ¹⁷ For if I do this willingly, I have a reward, but if unwillingly, I am entrusted with a commission. ¹⁸ What then is my reward? To preach the gospel and offer it free of charge and not make full use of my rights in the gospel.

✱ ¹⁹ Although I am free from all and not anyone's slave, I have made myself a slave to everyone, in order to win more people. ²⁰ To the Jews I became like a Jew, to win Jews; to those under the law, like one under the law—though I myself am not under the law—to win those under the law. ²¹ To those who are without the law, like one without the law—though I am not without God's law but under the law of Christ—to win those without the law. ²² To the weak I became weak, in order to win the weak. I have become all things to all people, so that I may by every possible means save some. ²³ Now I do all this because of the gospel, so that I may share in the blessings. ✱

²⁴ Don't you know that the runners in a stadium all race, but only one receives the prize? Run in such a way to win the prize. ²⁵ Now everyone who competes exercises self-control in everything. They do it to receive a perishable crown, but we an imperishable crown. ²⁶ So I do not run like one who runs aimlessly or box like one beating the air. ²⁷ Instead, I discipline my body and bring it under strict control, so that after preaching to others, I myself will not be disqualified.

MATTHEW 15:11

"It's not what goes into the mouth that defiles a person, but what comes out of the mouth—this defiles a person."

ROMANS 15:17-19

¹⁷ Therefore I have reason to boast in Christ Jesus regarding what pertains to God. ¹⁸ For I would not dare say anything except what Christ has accomplished through me by word and deed for the obedience of the Gentiles, ¹⁹ by the power of miraculous signs and wonders, and by the power of God's Spirit. As a result, I have fully proclaimed the gospel of Christ from Jerusalem all the way around to Illyricum.

9-7-18

DAY 12

Warnings from Israel's Past

1 CORINTHIANS 10
WARNINGS FROM ISRAEL'S PAST

[1] Now I do not want you to be unaware, brothers and sisters, that our ancestors were all under the cloud, all passed through the sea, [2] and all were baptized into Moses in the cloud and in the sea. [3] They all ate the same spiritual food, [4] and all drank the same spiritual drink. For they drank from the spiritual rock that followed them, and that rock was Christ. [5] Nevertheless God was not pleased with most of them, since they were struck down in the wilderness.

[6] Now these things took place as examples for us, so that we will not desire evil things as they did. [7] Don't become idolaters as some of them were; as it is written, The people sat down to eat and drink, and got up to party. [8] Let us not commit sexual immorality as some of them did, and in a single day twenty-three thousand people died. [9] Let us not test Christ as some of them did and were destroyed by snakes. [10] And don't complain as some of them did, and were killed by the destroyer. [11] These things happened to them as examples, and they were written for our instruction, on whom the ends of the ages have come. [12] So, whoever thinks he stands must be careful not to fall. [13] No temptation has come upon you except what is common to humanity. But God is faithful; he will not allow you to be tempted beyond what you are able, but with the temptation he will also provide a way out so that you may be able to bear it.

WARNING AGAINST IDOLATRY

[14] So then, my dear friends, flee from idolatry. [15] I am speaking as to sensible people. Judge for yourselves what I am saying. [16] The cup of blessing that we bless, is it not a sharing in the blood of Christ? The bread that we break, is it not a sharing in the body of Christ? [17] Because there is one bread, we who are many are one body, since all of us share the one bread. [18] Consider the people of Israel. Do not those who eat the sacrifices participate in the altar? [19] What am I saying then? That food sacrificed to idols is anything, or that

CONTINUED

NO ONE IS TO SEEK
HIS OWN GOOD,
BUT THE GOOD OF
THE OTHER PERSON.

1 CORINTHIANS 10:24

an idol is anything? [20] No, but I do say that what they sacrifice, they sacrifice to demons and not to God. I do not want you to be participants with demons! [21] You cannot drink the cup of the Lord and the cup of demons. You cannot share in the Lord's table and the table of demons. [22] Or are we provoking the Lord to jealousy? Are we stronger than he?

CHRISTIAN LIBERTY

[23] "Everything is permissible," but not everything is beneficial. "Everything is permissible," but not everything builds up. [24] No one is to seek his own good, but the good of the other person.

[25] Eat everything that is sold in the meat market, without raising questions for the sake of conscience, [26] since the earth is the Lord's, and all that is in it. [27] If any of the unbelievers invites you over and you want to go, eat everything that is set before you, without raising questions for the sake of conscience. [28] But if someone says to you, "This is food from a sacrifice," do not eat it, out of consideration for the one who told you, and for the sake of conscience. [29] I do not mean your own conscience, but the other person's. For why is my freedom judged by another person's conscience? [30] If I partake with thanksgiving, why am I criticized because of something for which I give thanks?

[31] So, whether you eat or drink, or whatever you do, do everything for the glory of God. [32] Give no offense to Jews or Greeks or the church of God, [33] just as I also try to please everyone in everything, not seeking my own benefit, but the benefit of many, so that they may be saved.

1 CORINTHIANS 11:1

Imitate me, as I also imitate Christ.

EXODUS 13:17-22

THE ROUTE OF THE EXODUS

[17] When Pharaoh let the people go, God did not lead them along the road to the land of the Philistines, even though it was nearby; for God said, "The people will change their minds and return to Egypt if they face war." [18] So he led the people around toward the Red Sea along the road of the wilderness. And the Israelites left the land of Egypt in battle formation.

[19] Moses took the bones of Joseph with him, because Joseph had made the Israelites swear a solemn oath, saying, "God will certainly come to your aid; then you must take my bones with you from this place."

[20] They set out from Succoth and camped at Etham on the edge of the wilderness. [21] The LORD went ahead of them in a pillar of cloud to lead them on their way during the day and in a pillar of fire to give them light at night, so that they could travel day or night. [22] The pillar of cloud by day and the pillar of fire by night never left its place in front of the people.

PHILIPPIANS 2:1-2
CHRISTIAN HUMILITY

[1] If then there is any encouragement in Christ, if any consolation of love, if any fellowship with the Spirit, if any affection and mercy, [2] make my joy complete by thinking the same way, having the same love, united in spirit, intent on one purpose.

Marshmallow Fruit Dip

INGREDIENTS: 3 | MAKES: 1 BOWL

1

1 (8-OUNCE)
PACKAGE CREAM CHEESE,
SOFTENED

2

1 (7-OUNCE)
JAR MARSHMALLOW
CREAM

3

½ CUP
POWDERED SUGAR

OTHER

STRAWBERRIES

BLACKBERRIES

BLUEBERRIES

LONG SKEWERS

DIRECTIONS

Combine all ingredients by hand or with a mixer.

Store dip in refrigerator until ready to serve.

WE LOVE SERVING
FRUIT ON SKEWERS!

GRACE DAY

Use this day to pray, rest, and reflect on
this week's reading, giving thanks for the
grace that is ours in Christ.

*Nevertheless, God's solid
foundation stands firm, bearing
this inscription: The Lord knows
those who are his, and let everyone
who calls on the name of the Lord
turn away from wickedness.*

2 TIMOTHY 2:19

WEEKLY TRUTH

Scripture is God-breathed and true. When we memorize it, we carry the gospel with us wherever we go.

This week's verse is a reminder that Christ's sacrifice for us includes our entire self.

Don't you know that your body is a temple of the Holy Spirit who is in you, whom you have from God? You are not your own, for you were bought at a price. So glorify God with your body.

1 CORINTHIANS 6:19-20

Find the corresponding memory card in the back of this book.

Week Three

DAY 15

The Lord's Supper

1 CORINTHIANS 11:2-34
INSTRUCTIONS ABOUT HEAD COVERINGS

[2] Now I praise you because you remember me in everything and hold fast to the traditions just as I delivered them to you. [3] But I want you to know that Christ is the head of every man, and the man is the head of the woman, and God is the head of Christ. [4] Every man who prays or prophesies with something on his head dishonors his head. [5] Every woman who prays or prophesies with her head uncovered dishonors her head, since that is one and the same as having her head shaved. [6] For if a woman doesn't cover her head, she should have her hair cut off. But if it is disgraceful for a woman to have her hair cut off or her head shaved, let her head be covered.

[7] A man should not cover his head, because he is the image and glory of God. So too, woman is the glory of man. [8] For man did not come from woman, but woman came from man. [9] Neither was man created for the sake of woman, but woman for the sake of man. [10] This is why a woman should

have a symbol of authority on her head, because of the angels. [11] In the Lord, however, woman is not independent of man, and man is not independent of woman. [12] For just as woman came from man, so man comes through woman, and all things come from God.

[13] Judge for yourselves: Is it proper for a woman to pray to God with her head uncovered? [14] Does not even nature itself teach you that if a man has long hair it is a disgrace to him, [15] but that if a woman has long hair, it is her glory? For her hair is given to her as a covering. [16] If anyone wants to argue about this, we have no other custom, nor do the churches of God.

THE LORD'S SUPPER

[17] Now in giving this instruction I do not praise you, since you come together not for the better but for the worse. [18] For to begin with, I hear that when you come together as a church there are divisions among you, and in part I believe it. [19] Indeed, it is necessary that there be factions among you, so that those who are approved may be recognized among you. [20] When you come together, then, it is not to eat the Lord's Supper. [21] For at the meal, each one eats his own supper. So one person is hungry while another gets drunk! [22] Don't you have homes in which to eat and drink? Or do you despise the church of God and humiliate those who have nothing? What should I say to you? Should I praise you? I do not praise you in this matter!

[23] For I received from the Lord what I also passed on to you: On the night when he was betrayed, the Lord Jesus took bread, [24] and when he had given thanks, broke it, and said, "This is my body, which is for you. Do this in remembrance of me."

[25] In the same way also he took the cup, after supper, and said, "This cup is the new covenant in my blood. Do this, as often as you drink it, in remembrance of me." [26] For as often as you eat this bread and drink the cup, you proclaim the Lord's death until he comes.

SELF-EXAMINATION

[27] So then, whoever eats the bread or drinks the cup of the Lord in an unworthy manner will be guilty of sin against the body and blood of the Lord. [28] Let a person examine himself; in this way let him eat the bread and drink from the cup. [29] For whoever eats and drinks without recognizing the body, eats and drinks judgment on himself. [30] This is why many are sick and ill among you, and many have fallen asleep. [31] If we were properly judging ourselves, we would not be judged, [32] but when we are judged by the Lord, we are disciplined, so that we may not be condemned with the world.

[33] Therefore, my brothers and sisters, when you come together to eat, welcome one another. [34] If anyone is hungry, he should eat at home, so that when you gather

together you will not come under judgment. I will give instructions about the other matters whenever I come.

MATTHEW 26:26-28
THE FIRST LORD'S SUPPER

26 As they were eating, Jesus took bread, blessed and broke it, gave it to the disciples, and said, "Take and eat it; this is my body." 27 Then he took a cup, and after giving thanks, he gave it to them and said, "Drink from it, all of you.

28 For this is my blood of the covenant, which is poured out for many for the forgiveness of sins."

ROMANS 3:25-26

25 God presented him as an atoning sacrifice in his blood, received through faith, to demonstrate his righteousness, because in his restraint God passed over the sins previously committed. 26 God presented him to demonstrate his righteousness at the present time, so that he would be righteous and declare righteous the one who has faith in Jesus.

The Lord's Supper

The Lord's Supper is a sacrament—an outward, visible sign of an inward,
spiritual reality which Jesus commands the Church to observe (Lk 22:19).
Here's a look at what Scripture teaches about the Lord's Supper.

known as	origin	frequency

THE LORD'S SUPPER
1 CORINTHIANS 11:20

ESTABLISHED BY JESUS
"Jesus took bread, blessed and broke it…"
MATTHEW 26:26

PRECISE FREQUENCY UNSPECIFIED
"For as often as you eat this bread and drink the cup…"
1 CORINTHIANS 11:26

THE LORD'S TABLE
1 CORINTHIANS 10:21

INTRODUCED DURING PASSOVER
"…they prepared the Passover."
MARK 14:16

REGULARLY
"When you come together…"
1 CORINTIHIANS 11:20

BREAKING OF BREAD
ACTS 2:42; 20:7

TOOK PLACE ON MAUNDY THURSDAY
"On the night when he was betrayed…"
1 CORINTHIANS 11:23

ONGOING
"…you proclaim the Lord's death until he comes."
1 CORINTHIANS 11:26

COMMUNION
Sharing in the body of Christ
1 CORINTHIANS 10:16

SHARED WITH JESUS' DISCIPLES
"…he took bread…gave it to them…"
LUKE 22:19

HISTORICALLY, ON SUNDAY
"On the first day of the week, we assembled to break bread."
ACTS 20:7

EUCHARIST
Giving thanks
1 CORINTHIANS 11:24

CONSISTED OF UNLEAVENED BREAD AND PASSOVER WINE
"…he took bread…then he took a cup…"
MARK 14:22-23

THE LOVE FEAST
2 PETER 2:13; JUDE 12

purpose

instruction and warning

TO SYMBOLIZE CHRIST'S SACRIFICE

"Jesus took bread…and said…'this is my body.' Then he took a cup…and said, '…this is my blood of the covenant, which is poured out for many for the forgiveness of sins.'"

MATTHEW 26:26-28

TO REMIND US OF CHRIST'S SACRIFICE

"This is my body, which is given for you. Do this in remembrance of me."

LUKE 22:19

FOR JESUS TO REASSIGN THE MEANING OF THE PASSOVER, SHOWING HIMSELF AS THE PERFECT PASSOVER LAMB

"This cup is the new covenant in my blood, which is poured out for you."

LUKE 22:20

FOR THE CHURCH TO COMMUNE WITH CHRIST

"…where two or three are gathered together in my name, I am there among them."

MATTHEW 18:20

FOR THE CHURCH TO COMMUNE WITH ONE ANOTHER

"…when you come together to eat, welcome one another."

1 CORINTHIANS 11:33

FOR THE CHURCH TO BEAR WITNESS PUBLICLY TO CHRIST

"…you proclaim the Lord's death until he comes."

1 CORINTHIANS 11:26

COME IN A POSTURE OF HUMILITY

"…do you despise the church of God and humiliate those who have nothing?"

1 CORINTHIANS 11:22

USE THE TIME TO CONFESS SIN

"Let a person examine himself…. For whoever eats and drinks without recognizing the body, eats and drinks judgment on himself."

1 CORINTHIANS 11:28-29

TREAT THE LORD'S SUPPER AS SACRED

"…whoever eats the bread or drinks the cup of the Lord in an unworthy manner will be guilty of sin against the body and blood of the Lord."

1 CORINTHIANS 11:27

GOD MAY DISCIPLINE THOSE WHO DISHONOR THE LORD'S TABLE

"…when we are judged by the Lord, we are disciplined…"

1 CORINTHIANS 11:32

9-15-18

DAY 16

Unity and Diversity in the Body

1 CORINTHIANS 12
DIVERSITY OF SPIRITUAL GIFTS

¹ Now concerning spiritual gifts: brothers and sisters, I do not want you to be unaware. ² You know that when you were pagans, you used to be enticed and led astray by mute idols. ³ Therefore I want you to know that no one speaking by the Spirit of God says, "Jesus is cursed," and no one can say, "Jesus is Lord," except by the Holy Spirit.

> ⁴ *Now there are different gifts, but the same Spirit.* ⁵ *There are different ministries, but the same Lord.*

⁶ And there are different activities, but the same God produces each gift in each person. ⁷ A manifestation of the Spirit is given to each person for the common good: ⁸ to one is given a message of wisdom through the Spirit, to another, a message of knowledge by the same Spirit, ⁹ to another, faith by the same Spirit, to another, gifts of healing by the one Spirit, ¹⁰ to another, the performing of miracles, to another, prophecy, to another, distinguishing between spirits, to another, different kinds of tongues, to another, interpretation of tongues. ¹¹ One and the same Spirit is active in all these, distributing to each person as he wills.

UNITY YET DIVERSITY IN THE BODY

¹² For just as the body is one and has many parts, and all the parts of that body, though many, are one body—so also is Christ. ¹³ For we were all baptized by one Spirit into one body—whether Jews or Greeks, whether slaves or free—and we were all given one Spirit to drink. ¹⁴ Indeed, the body is not one part but many. ¹⁵ If the foot should say, "Because I'm not a hand, I don't belong to the body," it is not for that reason any less a part of the body. ¹⁶ And if the ear should say, "Because I'm not an eye, I don't belong to the body," it is not for that reason any less a part of the body. ¹⁷ If the

STUDY QUESTIONS ON P. 158

whole body were an eye, where would the hearing be? If the whole body were an ear, where would the sense of smell be? [18] But as it is, God has arranged each one of the parts in the body just as he wanted. [19] And if they were all the same part, where would the body be? [20] As it is, there are many parts, but one body. [21] The eye cannot say to the hand, "I don't need you!" Or again, the head can't say to the feet, "I don't need you!" [22] On the contrary, those parts of the body that are weaker are indispensable. [23] And those parts of the body that we consider less honorable, we clothe these with greater honor, and our unrespectable parts are treated with greater respect, [24] which our respectable parts do not need.

Instead, God has put the body together, giving greater honor to the less honorable, [25] so that there would be no division in the body, but that the members would have the same concern for each other. [26] So if one member suffers, all the members suffer with it; if one member is honored, all the members rejoice with it.

[27] Now you are the body of Christ, and individual members of it. [28] And God has appointed these in the church: first apostles, second prophets, third teachers, next miracles, then gifts of healing, helping, administrating, various kinds of tongues. [29] Are all apostles? Are all prophets? Are all teachers? Do all do miracles? [30] Do all have gifts of healing? Do all speak in other tongues? Do all interpret? [31] But desire the greater gifts. And I will show you an even better way.

ROMANS 12:4-5

[4] Now as we have many parts in one body, and all the parts do not have the same function, [5] in the same way we who are many are one body in Christ and individually members of one another.

1 THESSALONIANS 5:19-21

[19] Don't stifle the Spirit. [20] Don't despise prophecies, [21] but test all things. Hold on to what is good.

DAY 17

Love, the Superior Way

1 CORINTHIANS 13
LOVE: THE SUPERIOR WAY

[1] If I speak human or angelic tongues but do not have love, I am a noisy gong or a clanging cymbal. [2] If I have the gift of prophecy and understand all mysteries and all knowledge, and if I have all faith so that I can move mountains but do not have love, I am nothing. [3] And if I give away all my possessions, and if I give over my body in order to boast but do not have love, I gain nothing.

[4] Love is patient, love is kind. Love does not envy, is not boastful, is not arrogant, [5] is not rude, is not self-seeking, is not irritable, and does not keep a record of wrongs.

[6] Love finds no joy in unrighteousness but rejoices in the truth.

[7] It bears all things, believes all things, hopes all things, endures all things.

[8] Love never ends. But as for prophecies, they will come to an end; as for tongues, they will cease; as for knowledge, it will come to an end. [9] For we know in part, and we prophesy in part, [10] but when the perfect comes, the partial will come to an end. [11] When I was a child, I spoke like a child, I thought like a child, I reasoned like a child. When I became a man, I put aside childish things. [12] For now we see only a reflection as in a mirror, but then face to face. Now I know in part, but then I will know fully, as I am fully known. [13] Now these three remain: faith, hope, and love—but the greatest of these is love.

EZEKIEL 20:35

I will lead you into the wilderness of the peoples and enter into judgment with you there face to face.

GALATIANS 5:5-26

[5] For we eagerly await through the Spirit, by faith, the hope of righteousness. [6] For in Christ Jesus neither circumcision nor uncircumcision accomplishes anything; what matters is faith working through love.

[7] You were running well. Who prevented you from being persuaded regarding the truth? [8] This persuasion does not come from the one who calls you. [9] A little leaven leavens the whole batch of dough. [10] I myself am persuaded in the Lord you will not accept any other view. But whoever it is that is confusing you will pay the penalty. [11] Now brothers and sisters, if I still preach circumcision, why am I still persecuted? In that case the offense of the cross has been abolished. [12] I wish those who are disturbing you might also let themselves be mutilated!

[13] For you were called to be free, brothers and sisters; only don't use this freedom as an opportunity for the flesh, but serve one another through love. [14] For the whole law is fulfilled in one statement: Love your neighbor as yourself. [15] But if you bite and devour one another, watch out, or you will be consumed by one another.

THE SPIRIT VERSUS THE FLESH

[16] I say then, walk by the Spirit and you will certainly not carry out the desire of the flesh. [17] For the flesh desires what is against the Spirit, and the Spirit desires what is against the flesh; these are opposed to each other, so that you don't do what you want. [18] But if you are led by the Spirit, you are not under the law.

[19] Now the works of the flesh are obvious: sexual immorality, moral impurity, promiscuity, [20] idolatry, sorcery, hatreds, strife, jealousy, outbursts of anger, selfish ambitions, dissensions, factions, [21] envy, drunkenness, carousing, and anything similar. I am warning you about these things—as I warned you before—that those who practice such things will not inherit the kingdom of God.

[22] But the fruit of the Spirit is love, joy, peace, patience, kindness, goodness, faithfulness, [23] gentleness, and self-control. The law is not against such things. [24] Now those who belong to Christ Jesus have crucified the flesh with its passions and desires. [25] If we live by the Spirit, let us also keep in step with the Spirit. [26] Let us not become conceited, provoking one another, envying one another.

Gifts from the Holy Spirit

1 CORINTHIANS 14
PROPHECY: A SUPERIOR GIFT

[1] Pursue love and desire spiritual gifts, and especially that you may prophesy. [2] For the person who speaks in another tongue is not speaking to people but to God, since no one understands him; he speaks mysteries in the Spirit. [3] On the other hand, the person who prophesies speaks to people for their strengthening, encouragement, and consolation. [4] The person who speaks in another tongue builds himself up, but the one who prophesies builds up the church. [5] I wish all of you spoke in other tongues, but even more that you prophesied. The person who prophesies is greater than the person who speaks in tongues, unless he interprets so that the church may be built up.

[6] So now, brothers and sisters, if I come to you speaking in other tongues, how will I benefit you unless I speak to you with a revelation or knowledge or prophecy or teaching? [7] Even lifeless instruments that produce sounds—whether flute or harp—if they don't make a distinction in the notes, how will what is played on the flute or harp be recognized? [8] In fact, if the bugle makes an unclear sound, who will prepare for battle? [9] In the same way, unless you use your tongue for intelligible speech, how will what is spoken be known? For you will be speaking into the air. [10] There are doubtless many different kinds of languages in the world, none is without meaning. [11] Therefore, if I do not know the meaning of the language, I will be a foreigner to the speaker, and the speaker will be a foreigner to me. [12] So also you—since you are zealous for spiritual gifts, seek to excel in building up the church.

[13] Therefore the person who speaks in another tongue should pray that he can interpret. [14] For if I pray in another tongue, my spirit prays, but my understanding is unfruitful. [15] What then? I will pray with the spirit, and I will also pray with my understanding. I will sing praise with the spirit, and I will also sing praise with my understanding. [16] Otherwise, if you praise with the spirit, how will the outsider say "Amen" at your giving of thanks,

CONTINUED

SEEK TO EXCEL IN BUILDING UP THE CHURCH.

1 CORINTHIANS 14:12

since he does not know what you are saying? 17 For you may very well be giving thanks, but the other person is not being built up. 18 I thank God that I speak in other tongues more than all of you; 19 yet in the church I would rather speak five words with my understanding, in order to teach others also, than ten thousand words in another tongue.

20 Brothers and sisters, don't be childish in your thinking, but be infants in regard to evil and adult in your thinking. 21 It is written in the law,

> I will speak to this people
> by people of other tongues
> and by the lips of foreigners,
> and even then, they will not listen to me,

says the Lord. 22 Speaking in other tongues, then, is intended as a sign, not for believers but for unbelievers, while prophecy is not for unbelievers but for believers. 23 If, therefore, the whole church assembles together and all are speaking in other tongues and people who are outsiders or unbelievers come in, will they not say that you are out of your minds? 24 But if all are prophesying and some unbeliever or outsider comes in, he is convicted by all and is called to account by all. 25 The secrets of his heart will be revealed, and as a result he will fall facedown and worship God, proclaiming, "God is really among you."

ORDER IN CHURCH MEETINGS

26 What then, brothers and sisters? Whenever you come together, each one has a hymn, a teaching, a revelation, another tongue, or an interpretation.

Everything is to be done for building up.

27 If anyone speaks in another tongue, there are to be only two, or at the most three, each in turn, and let someone interpret. 28 But if there is no interpreter, that person is to keep silent in the church and speak to himself and God. 29 Two or three prophets should speak, and the others should evaluate. 30 But if something has been revealed to another person sitting there, the first prophet should be silent. 31 For you can all prophesy one by one, so that everyone may learn and everyone may be encouraged. 32 And the prophets' spirits are subject to the prophets, 33 since God is not a God of disorder but of peace.

As in all the churches of the saints, 34 the women should be silent in the churches, for they are not permitted to speak, but are to submit themselves, as the law also says. 35 If they want to learn something, let them ask their own husbands at home, since it is disgraceful for a woman to speak in the church. 36 Or did the word of God originate from you, or did it come to you only?

37 If anyone thinks he is a prophet or spiritual, he should recognize that what I write to you is the Lord's command. 38 If anyone ignores this, he will be ignored. 39 So then, my brothers and sisters, be eager to prophesy, and do not forbid speaking in other tongues. 40 But everything is to be done decently and in order.

EXODUS 25:8

"They are to make a sanctuary for me so that I may dwell among them."

1 JOHN 4:1-3

1 Dear friends, do not believe every spirit, but test the spirits to see if they are from God, because many false prophets have gone out into the world.

2 This is how you know the Spirit of God: Every spirit that confesses that Jesus Christ has come in the flesh is from God, 3 but every spirit that does not confess Jesus is not from God. This is the spirit of the antichrist, which you have heard is coming; even now it is already in the world.

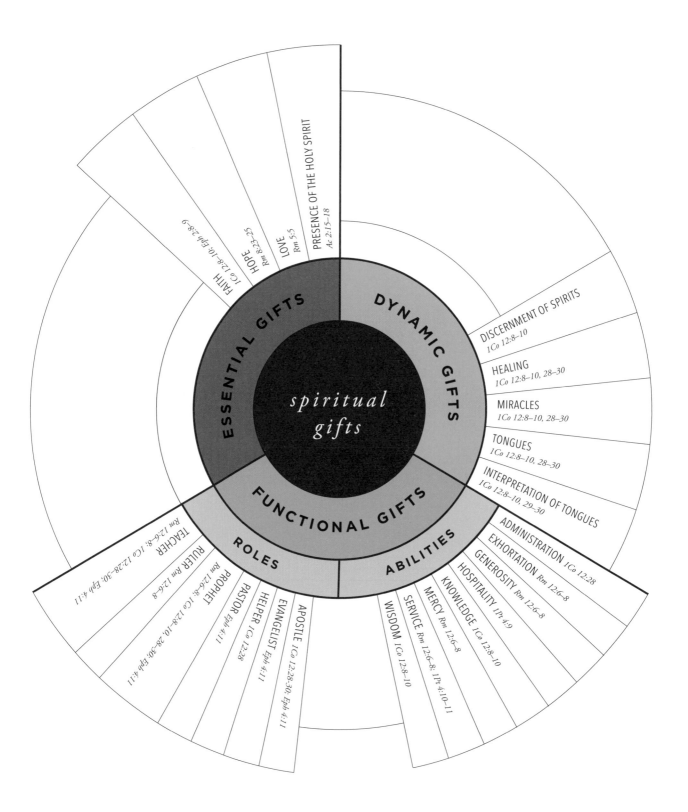

spiritual gifts

ESSENTIAL GIFTS

DYNAMIC GIFTS

FUNCTIONAL GIFTS

ROLES

ABILITIES

PRESENCE OF THE HOLY SPIRIT
Ac 2:15–18

LOVE
Rm 5:5

HOPE
1Co 12:8–10; Eph 2:8–9

FAITH
1Co 12:8–10; Eph 2:8–9

DISCERNMENT OF SPIRITS
1Co 12:8–10

HEALING
1Co 12:8–10, 28–30

MIRACLES
1Co 12:8–10, 28–30

TONGUES
1Co 12:8–10, 28–30

INTERPRETATION OF TONGUES
1Co 12:8–10, 29–30

ADMINISTRATION *1Co 12:28*

EXHORTATION *Rm 12:6–8*

GENEROSITY *Rm 12:6–8*

HOSPITALITY *1Pt 4:9*

KNOWLEDGE *1Co 12:8–10*

MERCY *Rm 12:6–8; 1Pt 4:10–11*

SERVICE *Rm 12:6–8*

WISDOM *1Co 12:8–10*

APOSTLE *1Co 12:28–30; Eph 4:11*

EVANGELIST *Eph 4:11*

HELPER *1Co 12:28*

PASTOR *Eph 4:11*

PROPHET *Rm 12:6–8; 1Co 12:8–10, 28–30; Eph 4:11*

RULER *Rm 12:6–8*

TEACHER *Rm 12:6–8; 1Co 12:28–30; Eph 4:11*

Spiritual gifts are one way God equips the Church for the life and work He calls us to. These gifts range from essentials for the Christian life, to miraculous abilities, to roles and skills necessary for the ongoing ministry of the Church. While the gifts shown here vary in type, they all share one distinctive quality: they come directly from the Holy Spirit.

ESSENTIAL GIFTS:

QUALITIES GIVEN TO ALL BELIEVERS EVERYWHERE WHICH ARE NECESSARY FOR LIVING THE CHRISTIAN LIFE

DYNAMIC GIFTS:

SPECIAL ABILITIES GIVEN BY THE HOLY SPIRIT FOR THE SPECIFIC PURPOSE OF DELIVERING OR VALIDATING A MESSAGE FROM GOD

FUNCTIONAL GIFTS:

ROLES AND ABILITIES NEEDED FOR THE ONGOING STRUCTURE AND MINISTRY OF THE CHURCH ON EARTH

Many scholars believe that the dynamic gifts centering around speaking for God ceased to be necessary—and therefore ceased to exist—once the Bible was complete.

DAY 19

Essential Resurrection

1 CORINTHIANS 15:1-19
RESURRECTION ESSENTIAL TO THE GOSPEL

[1] Now I want to make clear for you, brothers and sisters, the gospel I preached to you, which you received, on which you have taken your stand [2] and by which you are being saved, if you hold to the message I preached to you—unless you believed in vain. [3] For I passed on to you as most important what I also received: that Christ died for our sins according to the Scriptures, [4] that he was buried, that he was raised on the third day according to the Scriptures, [5] and that he appeared to Cephas, then to the Twelve. [6] Then he appeared to over five hundred brothers and sisters at one time; most of them are still alive, but some have fallen asleep. [7] Then he appeared to James, then to all the apostles. [8] Last of all, as to one born at the wrong time, he also appeared to me.

[9] For I am the least of the apostles, not worthy to be called an apostle, because I persecuted the church of God. [10] But by the grace of God I am what I am, and his grace toward me was not in vain. On the contrary, I worked harder than any of them, yet not I, but the grace of God that was with me. [11] Whether, then, it is I or they, so we proclaim and so you have believed.

RESURRECTION ESSENTIAL TO THE FAITH

[12] Now if Christ is proclaimed as raised from the dead, how can some of you say, "There is no resurrection of the dead"? [13] If there is no resurrection of the dead, then not even Christ has been raised;

[14] *and if Christ has not been raised, then our proclamation is in vain, and so is your faith.*

[15] Moreover, we are found to be false witnesses about God, because we have testified wrongly about God that he raised up Christ—whom he

did not raise up, if in fact the dead are not raised. [16] For if the dead are not raised, not even Christ has been raised. [17] And if Christ has not been raised, your faith is worthless; you are still in your sins. [18] Those, then, who have fallen asleep in Christ have also perished. [19] If we have put our hope in Christ for this life only, we should be pitied more than anyone.

EPHESIANS 2:4-7

[4] But God, who is rich in mercy, because of his great love that he had for us, [5] made us alive with Christ even though we were dead in trespasses. You are saved by grace! [6] He also raised us up with him and seated us with him in the heavens in Christ Jesus, [7] so that in the coming ages he might display the immeasurable riches of his grace through his kindness to us in Christ Jesus.

HEBREWS 2:5-9

JESUS AND HUMANITY

[5] For he has not subjected to angels the world to come that we are talking about. [6] But someone somewhere has testified:

What is man that you remember him,
or the son of man that you care for him?
[7] You made him lower than the angels
for a short time;
you crowned him with glory and honor
[8] and subjected everything under his feet.

For in subjecting everything to him, he left nothing that is not subject to him. As it is, we do not yet see everything subjected to him. [9] But we do see Jesus—made lower than the angels for a short time so that by God's grace he might taste death for everyone—crowned with glory and honor because he suffered death.

Citrus and Thyme Refresher

INGREDIENTS: 4 | MAKES: 6 DRINKS

1

6 CUPS
GRAPEFRUIT JUICE

2

3 CUPS
ORANGE JUICE

3

6 TABLESPOONS
LIME JUICE

4

1½ CUPS
CLUB SODA

FOR GARNISH

FLAKE SALT OR SUGAR

FRESH THYME SPRIGS

ICE

DIRECTIONS

Salt or sugar the rims of six glasses. Combine grapefruit juice, orange juice, and lime juice in a small pitcher. Divide evenly among ice-filled glasses. Top with club soda and garnish with a sprig of fresh thyme.

GRACE DAY

Use this day to pray, rest, and reflect on this week's reading, giving thanks for the grace that is ours in Christ.

But God, who is rich in mercy, because of his great love that he had for us, made us alive with Christ even though we were dead in trespasses. You are saved by grace!

EPHESIANS 2:4-5

Scripture is God-breathed and true. When we memorize it, we carry the gospel with us wherever we go.

This week's verse describes the unity we have in the Spirit.

Now there are different gifts, but the same Spirit.

1 CORINTHIANS 12:4

Find the corresponding memory card in the back of this book.

Week Four

Victorious Resurrection

1 CORINTHIANS 15:20-58

CHRIST'S RESURRECTION GUARANTEES OURS

20 But as it is, Christ has been raised from the dead, the firstfruits of those who have fallen asleep. 21 For since death came through a man, the resurrection of the dead also comes through a man. 22 For just as in Adam all die, so also in Christ all will be made alive.

23 But each in his own order: Christ, the firstfruits; afterward, at his coming, those who belong to Christ. 24 Then comes the end, when he hands over the kingdom to God the Father, when he abolishes all rule and all authority and power. 25 For he must reign until he puts all his enemies under his feet. 26 The last enemy to be abolished is death. 27 For God has put everything under his feet. Now when it says "everything" is put under him, it is obvious that he who puts everything under him is the exception. 28 When everything is subject to Christ, then the Son himself will also be subject to the one who subjected everything to him, so that God may be all in all.

RESURRECTION SUPPORTED BY CHRISTIAN EXPERIENCE

29 Otherwise what will they do who are being baptized for the dead? If the dead are not raised at all, then why are people baptized for them? 30 Why are we in danger every hour? 31 I face death every day, as surely as I may boast about you, brothers and sisters, in Christ Jesus our Lord. 32 If I fought wild beasts in Ephesus as a mere man, what good did that do me? If the dead are not raised, Let us eat and drink, for tomorrow we die. 33 Do not be deceived: "Bad company corrupts good morals." 34 Come to your senses and stop sinning; for some people are ignorant about God. I say this to your shame.

THE NATURE OF THE RESURRECTION BODY

35 But someone will ask, "How are the dead raised? What kind of body will they have when they come?" 36 You fool! What you sow does not come to life unless it dies. 37 And as for what you sow— you are not sowing the body that will be, but only a seed, perhaps of wheat or another grain.

"Fruity," Mixed media on canvas, 22x28

³⁸ But God gives it a body as he wants, and to each of the seeds its own body. ³⁹ Not all flesh is the same flesh; there is one flesh for humans, another for animals, another for birds, and another for fish. ⁴⁰ There are heavenly bodies and earthly bodies, but the splendor of the heavenly bodies is different from that of the earthly ones. ⁴¹ There is a splendor of the sun, another of the moon, and another of the stars; in fact, one star differs from another star in splendor. ⁴² So it is with the resurrection of the dead:

Sown in corruption, raised in incorruption; ⁴³ sown in dishonor, raised in glory; sown in weakness, raised in power; ⁴⁴ sown a natural body, raised a spiritual body.

If there is a natural body, there is also a spiritual body. ⁴⁵ So it is written, The first man Adam became a living being; the last Adam became a life-giving spirit. ⁴⁶ However, the spiritual is not first, but the natural, then the spiritual.

⁴⁷ The first man was from the earth, a man of dust; the second man is from heaven. ⁴⁸ Like the man of dust, so are those who are of the dust; like the man of heaven, so are those who are of heaven. ⁴⁹ And just as we have borne the image of the man of dust, we will also bear the image of the man of heaven.

STUDY
QUESTIONS
ON P. 160

VICTORIOUS RESURRECTION

⁵⁰ What I am saying, brothers and sisters, is this: Flesh and blood cannot inherit the kingdom of God, nor can corruption inherit incorruption. ⁵¹ Listen, I am telling you a mystery: We will not all fall asleep, but we will all be changed, ⁵² in a moment, in the twinkling of an eye, at the last trumpet. For the trumpet will sound, and the dead will be raised incorruptible, and we will be changed. ⁵³ For this corruptible body must be clothed with incorruptibility, and this mortal body must be clothed with immortality. ⁵⁴ When this corruptible body is clothed with incorruptibility, and this mortal body is clothed with immortality, then the saying that is written will take place:

Death has been swallowed up in victory.
⁵⁵ Where, death, is your victory?
Where, death, is your sting?

⁵⁶ The sting of death is sin, and the power of sin is the law. ⁵⁷ But thanks be to God, who gives us the victory through our Lord Jesus Christ!

[58] Therefore, my dear brothers and sisters, be steadfast, immovable, always excelling in the Lord's work, because you know that your labor in the Lord is not in vain.

PHILIPPIANS 1:21

For me, to live is Christ and to die is gain.

1 THESSALONIANS 4:17

Then we who are still alive, who are left, will be caught up together with them in the clouds to meet the Lord in the air, and so we will always be with the Lord.

The Lord's Work

1 CORINTHIANS 16

COLLECTION FOR THE JERUSALEM CHURCH

[1] Now about the collection for the saints: Do the same as I instructed the Galatian churches. [2] On the first day of the week, each of you is to set something aside and save in keeping with how he is prospering, so that no collections will need to be made when I come. [3] When I arrive, I will send with letters those you recommend to carry your gift to Jerusalem. [4] If it is suitable for me to go as well, they will travel with me.

PAUL'S TRAVEL PLANS

[5] I will come to you after I pass through Macedonia—for I will be traveling through Macedonia— [6] and perhaps I will remain with you or even spend the winter, so that you may send me on my way wherever I go. [7] I don't want to see you now just in passing, since I hope to spend some time with you, if the Lord allows. [8] But I will stay in Ephesus until Pentecost, [9] because a wide door for effective ministry has opened for me—yet many oppose me. [10] If Timothy comes, see that he has nothing to fear while with you, because

he is doing the Lord's work, just as I am.

[11] So let no one look down on him. Send him on his way in peace so that he can come to me, because I am expecting him with the brothers.

[12] Now about our brother Apollos: I strongly urged him to come to you with the brothers, but he was not at all willing to come now. However, he will come when he has an opportunity.

FINAL EXHORTATION

[13] Be alert, stand firm in the faith, be courageous, be strong. [14] Do everything in love.

[15] Brothers and sisters, you know the household of Stephanas: They are the firstfruits of Achaia and have devoted themselves to serving the saints. I urge you [16] also to submit to such people, and to everyone who works and labors with them.

[17] I am delighted to have Stephanas, Fortunatus, and Achaicus present, because these men have made up for your absence. [18] For they have refreshed my spirit and yours. Therefore recognize such people.

CONCLUSION

[19] The churches of Asia send you greetings. Aquila and Priscilla send you greetings warmly in the Lord, along with the church that meets in their home. [20] All the brothers and sisters send you greetings. Greet one another with a holy kiss.

[21] This greeting is in my own hand—Paul. [22] If anyone does not love the Lord, a curse be on him. Our Lord, come! [23] The grace of the Lord Jesus be with you. [24] My love be with all of you in Christ Jesus.

LEVITICUS 23:15-22

[15] "You are to count seven complete weeks starting from the day after the Sabbath, the day you brought the sheaf of the presentation offering. [16] You are to count fifty days until the day after the seventh Sabbath and then present an offering of new grain to the Lord. [17] Bring two loaves of bread from your settlements as a presentation offering, each of them made from four quarts of fine flour, baked with yeast, as firstfruits to the Lord. [18] You are to present with the bread seven unblemished male lambs a year old, one young bull, and two rams. They will be a burnt offering to the Lord, with their grain offerings and drink offerings, a fire offering of a pleasing aroma to the Lord. [19] You are also to prepare one male goat as a sin offering, and two male lambs a year old as a fellowship sacrifice. [20] The priest will present the lambs with the bread of firstfruits as a presentation offering before the Lord; the bread and the two lambs will be holy to the Lord for the priest. [21] On that same day you are to make a proclamation and hold a sacred assembly. You are not to do any daily work. This is to be a permanent statute wherever you live throughout your generations. [22] When you reap the harvest of your land, you are not to reap all the way to the edge of your field or gather the gleanings of your harvest. Leave them for the poor and the resident alien; I am the Lord your God."

DEUTERONOMY 31:6-8

[6] "Be strong and courageous; don't be terrified or afraid of them. For the Lord your God is the one who will go with you; he will not leave you or abandon you."

[7] Moses then summoned Joshua and said to him in the sight of all Israel, "Be strong and courageous, for you will go with this people into the land the Lord swore to give to their fathers. You will enable them to take possession of it. [8] The Lord is the one who will go before you. He will be with you; he will not leave you or abandon you. Do not be afraid or discouraged."

second

2 CORINTHIANS

Key Verse

BUT HE SAID TO ME, "MY GRACE IS SUFFICIENT
FOR YOU, FOR MY POWER IS PERFECTED IN
WEAKNESS." THEREFORE, I WILL MOST GLADLY
BOAST ALL THE MORE ABOUT MY WEAKNESSES,
SO THAT CHRIST'S POWER MAY RESIDE IN ME.

2 CORINTHIANS 12:9

ON THE TIMELINE:

Paul wrote 2 Corinthians around AD 56, during his third missionary journey. He included more personal information about himself here than in any of his other letters.

A LITTLE BACKGROUND:

First Corinthians was not well received by the church at Corinth. Timothy had returned to Paul in Ephesus (1Co 4:17; 16:10) and reported that the church was still greatly troubled, in part due to the arrival of "false apostles" in Corinth (2Co 11:13–15). These were perhaps Judaizers, who asked Corinthian believers of Gentile heritage to live according to Mosaic regulations (Gl 2:14). Paul visited Corinth a second time, describing this visit as sorrowful or "painful" (2Co 2:1; 13:2).

Paul then wrote a third (now lost) severe letter of stinging rebuke to Corinth from Ephesus (2Co 2:3-4,9). After delivering the letter to Corinth, Titus came to Paul with the news that most of the Corinthian church had repented. Paul decided to write to them one more time, in the letter now known as 2 Corinthians, expressing his relief but still pleading with an unrepentant minority. He promised to come to Corinth a third time (2Co 12:14; 13:1), which he did while on his way to Jerusalem (Ac 20:2–3).

MESSAGE & PURPOSE:

Paul wrote to the Corinthian Christians to express his joy that the majority had been restored, to ask for an offering on behalf of the poor saints in Jerusalem, and to defend his ministry as an apostle to the minority of unrepentant Corinthian believers.

GIVE THANKS FOR THE
BOOK OF 2 CORINTHIANS:

Second Corinthians contributes to our understanding of ministry by teaching four key truths: God, in Christ, is reconciling the world to Himself and has given us a ministry of reconciliation; true ministry in Christ's name involves both suffering and victory; serving Christ means ministering in His name to every need of the people; and leaders in ministry need support and trust from those to whom they minister.

DAY 24

The God of Comfort

2 CORINTHIANS 1

GREETING

¹ Paul, an apostle of Christ Jesus by God's will, and Timothy our brother:

To the church of God at Corinth, with all the saints who are throughout Achaia.

² Grace to you and peace from God our Father and the Lord Jesus Christ.

THE GOD OF COMFORT

³ Blessed be the God and Father of our Lord Jesus Christ, the Father of mercies and the God of all comfort. ⁴ He comforts us in all our affliction, so that we may be able to comfort those who are in any kind of affliction, through the comfort we ourselves receive from God. ⁵ For just as the sufferings of Christ overflow to us, so also through Christ our comfort overflows. ⁶ If we are afflicted, it is for your comfort and salvation. If we are comforted, it is for your comfort, which produces in you patient endurance of the same sufferings that we suffer. ⁷ And our hope for you

is firm, because we know that as you share in the sufferings, so you will also share in the comfort.

⁸ We don't want you to be unaware, brothers and sisters, of our affliction that took place in Asia. We were completely overwhelmed—beyond our strength—so that we even despaired of life itself. ⁹ Indeed, we felt that we had received the sentence of death, so that we would not trust in ourselves but in God who raises the dead. ¹⁰ He has delivered us from such a terrible death, and he will deliver us. We have put our hope in him that he will deliver us again ¹¹ while you join in helping us by your prayers. Then many will give thanks on our behalf for the gift that came to us through the prayers of many.

A CLEAR CONSCIENCE

¹² Indeed, this is our boast: The testimony of our conscience is that we have conducted ourselves in the world, and especially toward you, with godly sincerity and purity, not by human wisdom but

CONTINUED

FOR JUST AS THE SUFFERINGS OF CHRIST OVERFLOW TO US, SO ALSO THROUGH CHRIST OUR COMFORT OVERFLOWS.

2 CORINTHIANS 1:5

by God's grace. ¹³ For we are writing nothing to you other than what you can read and also understand. I hope you will understand completely— ¹⁴ just as you have partially understood us—that we are your reason for pride, just as you also are ours in the day of our Lord Jesus.

A VISIT POSTPONED

¹⁵ Because of this confidence, I planned to come to you first, so that you could have a second benefit, ¹⁶ and to visit you on my way to Macedonia, and then come to you again from Macedonia and be helped by you on my journey to Judea. ¹⁷ Now when I planned this, was I of two minds? Or what I plan, do I plan in a purely human way so that I say "Yes, yes" and "No, no" at the same time? ¹⁸ As God is faithful, our message to you is not "Yes and no." ¹⁹ For the Son of God, Jesus Christ, whom we proclaimed among you—Silvanus, Timothy, and I—did not become "Yes and no." On the contrary, in him it is always "Yes."

²⁰ *For every one of God's promises is "Yes" in him.*

Therefore, through him we also say "Amen" to the glory of God. ²¹ Now it is God who strengthens us together with you in Christ, and who has anointed us. ²² He has also put his seal on us and given us the Spirit in our hearts as a down payment.

²³ I call on God as a witness, on my life, that it was to spare you that I did not come to Corinth. ²⁴ I do not mean that we lord it over your faith, but we are workers with you for your joy, because you stand firm in your faith.

2 CORINTHIANS 2:1-4

¹ In fact, I made up my mind about this: I would not come to you on another painful visit. ² For if I cause you pain, then who will cheer me other than the one being hurt by me? ³ I wrote this very thing so that when I came I wouldn't have pain from those who ought to give me joy, because I am confident about all of you that my joy will also be yours. ⁴ For I wrote to you with many tears out of an extremely troubled and anguished heart—not to cause you pain, but that you should know the abundant love I have for you.

ISAIAH 40:1-2

¹ "Comfort, comfort my people,"
says your God.
² "Speak tenderly to Jerusalem,
and announce to her
that her time of forced labor is over,
her iniquity has been pardoned,
and she has received from the LORD's hand
double for all her sins."

ROMANS 5:8-10

⁸ But God proves his own love for us in that while we were still sinners, Christ died for us. ⁹ How much more then, since we have now been declared righteous by his blood, will we be saved through him from wrath. ¹⁰ For if, while we were enemies, we were reconciled to God through the death of his Son, then how much more, having been reconciled, will we be saved by his life.

DAY 25

A Sinner Forgiven

2 CORINTHIANS 2:5-17

A SINNER FORGIVEN

⁵ If anyone has caused pain, he has caused pain not so much to me but to some degree—not to exaggerate—to all of you. ⁶ This punishment by the majority is sufficient for that person. ⁷ As a result, you should instead forgive and comfort him. Otherwise, he may be overwhelmed by excessive grief. ⁸ Therefore I urge you to reaffirm your love to him. ⁹ I wrote for this purpose: to test your character to see if you are obedient in everything. ¹⁰ Anyone you forgive, I do too. For what I have forgiven—if I have forgiven anything—it is for your benefit in the presence of Christ, ¹¹ so that we may not be taken advantage of by Satan. For we are not ignorant of his schemes.

A TRIP TO MACEDONIA

¹² When I came to Troas to preach the gospel of Christ, even though the Lord opened a door for me, ¹³ I had no rest in my spirit because I did not find my brother Titus. Instead, I said good-bye to them and left for Macedonia.

A MINISTRY OF LIFE OR DEATH

¹⁴ But thanks be to God, who always leads us in Christ's triumphal procession and through us spreads the aroma of the knowledge of him in every place. ¹⁵ For to God we are the fragrance of Christ among those who are being saved and among those who are perishing. ¹⁶ To some we are an aroma of death leading to death, but to others, an aroma of life leading to life. Who is adequate for these things? ¹⁷ For we do not market the word of God for profit like so many. On the contrary, we speak with sincerity in Christ, as from God and before God.

MATTHEW 6:14-15

¹⁴ "For if you forgive others their offenses, your heavenly Father will forgive you as well. ¹⁵ But if you don't forgive others, your Father will not forgive your offenses."

COLOSSIANS 3:12-17
THE CHRISTIAN LIFE

[12] Therefore, as God's chosen ones, holy and dearly loved, put on compassion, kindness, humility, gentleness, and patience, [13] bearing with one another and forgiving one another if anyone has a grievance against another. Just as the Lord has forgiven you, so you are also to forgive.

[14] *Above all, put on love, which is the perfect bond of unity.*

[15] And let the peace of Christ, to which you were also called in one body, rule your hearts. And be thankful. [16] Let the word of Christ dwell richly among you, in all wisdom teaching and admonishing one another through psalms, hymns, and spiritual songs, singing to God with gratitude in your hearts. [17] And whatever you do, in word or in deed, do everything in the name of the Lord Jesus, giving thanks to God the Father through him.

DAY 26

Living Letters

2 CORINTHIANS 3
LIVING LETTERS

¹ Are we beginning to commend ourselves again? Or do we need, like some, letters of recommendation to you or from you? ² You yourselves are our letter, written on our hearts, known and read by everyone. ³ You show that you are Christ's letter, delivered by us, not written with ink but with the Spirit of the living God—not on tablets of stone but on tablets of human hearts.

PAUL'S COMPETENCE

⁴ Such is the confidence we have through Christ before God. ⁵ It is not that we are competent in ourselves to claim anything as coming from ourselves, but our adequacy is from God. ⁶ He has made us competent to be ministers of a new covenant, not of the letter, but of the Spirit. For the letter kills, but the Spirit gives life.

NEW COVENANT MINISTRY

⁷ Now if the ministry that brought death, chiseled in letters on stones, came with glory, so that the Israelites were not able to gaze steadily at Moses's face because of its glory, which was set aside, ⁸ how will the ministry of the Spirit not be more glorious? ⁹ For if the ministry that brought condemnation had glory, the ministry that brings righteousness overflows with even more glory. ¹⁰ In fact, what had been glorious is not glorious now by comparison because of the glory that surpasses it. ¹¹ For if what was set aside was glorious, what endures will be even more glorious.

¹² Since, then, we have such a hope, we act with great boldness. ¹³ We are not like Moses, who used to put a veil over his face to prevent the Israelites from gazing steadily until the end of the glory of what was being set aside, ¹⁴ but their minds were hardened. For to this day, at the reading of the old covenant, the same veil remains; it is not lifted, because it is set aside only in Christ. ¹⁵ Yet still today, whenever Moses is read, a veil lies over their hearts, ¹⁶ but whenever a person turns to the Lord, the veil is removed.

¹⁷ Now the Lord is the Spirit, and where the Spirit of the Lord is, there is freedom.

¹⁸ We all, with unveiled faces, are looking as in a mirror at the glory of the Lord and are being transformed into the same image from glory to glory; this is from the Lord who is the Spirit.

JEREMIAH 31:31-34
THE NEW COVENANT

³¹ "Look, the days are coming"—this is the LORD's declaration—"when I will make a new covenant with the house of Israel and with the house of Judah. ³² This one will not be like the covenant I made with their ancestors on the day I took them by the hand to lead them out of the land of Egypt—my covenant that they broke even though I am their master"—the LORD's declaration. ³³ "Instead, this is the covenant I will make with the house of Israel after those days"—the LORD's declaration. "I will put my teaching within them and write it on their hearts. I will be their God, and they will be my people. ³⁴ No longer will one teach his neighbor or his brother, saying, 'Know the LORD,' for they will all know me, from the least to the greatest of them"—this is the LORD's declaration. "For I will forgive their iniquity and never again remember their sin."

1 JOHN 3:2
Dear friends, we are God's children now, and what we will be has not yet been revealed. We know that when he appears, we will be like him because we will see him as he is.

Butter-Dipped Radishes

INGREDIENTS: 3 | MAKES: 24 RADISHES

1

**2 BUNCHES
RADISHES**

2

**½ CUP
UNSALTED BUTTER**

3

**PINCH OF
FLEUR DE SEL
OR SEA SALT**

OTHER

WAX PAPER

DIRECTIONS

Rinse the radishes thoroughly with cold water, removing all dirt. Remove roots and trim stalks. Pat completely dry.

In a microwave-safe bowl, melt butter, whisking occasionally until smooth but still thick. Dip radishes in the butter. (Dip two or three times in the butter for a thicker coating.) Then dip in fleur de sel and place on a baking sheet lined with wax paper.

Let cool in the refrigerator until ready to serve.

LEAVING THE STALKS MAKES THIS
TREAT EASY TO SERVE UTENSIL-FREE

GRACE DAY

Use this day to pray, rest, and reflect on this week's reading, giving thanks for the grace that is ours in Christ.

"Be strong and courageous; don't be terrified or afraid of them. For the LORD your God is the one who will go with you; he will not leave you or abandon you."

DEUTERONOMY 31:6

WEEKLY TRUTH

Scripture is God-breathed and true. When we memorize it, we carry the gospel with us wherever we go.

This week's verse emphasizes our unity with Christ in both joy and sorrow.

For just as the sufferings of Christ overflow to us, so also through Christ our comfort overflows.

2 CORINTHIANS 1:5

Find the corresponding memory card in the back of this book.

Week Five

DAY 29

The Light of the Gospel

2 CORINTHIANS 4
THE LIGHT OF THE GOSPEL

[1] Therefore, since we have this ministry because we were shown mercy, we do not give up. [2] Instead, we have renounced secret and shameful things, not acting deceitfully or distorting the word of God, but commending ourselves before God to everyone's conscience by an open display of the truth. [3] But if our gospel is veiled, it is veiled to those who are perishing. [4] In their case, the god of this age has blinded the minds of the unbelievers to keep them from seeing the light of the gospel of the glory of Christ, who is the image of God. [5] For we are not proclaiming ourselves but Jesus Christ as Lord, and ourselves as your servants for Jesus's sake. [6] For God who said, "Let light shine out of darkness," has shone in our hearts to give the light of the knowledge of God's glory in the face of Jesus Christ.

TREASURE IN CLAY JARS

[7] Now we have this treasure in clay jars, so that this extraordinary power may be from God and not from us. [8] We are afflicted in every way but not crushed; we are perplexed but not in despair; [9] we are persecuted but not abandoned; we are struck down but not destroyed. [10] We always carry the death of Jesus in our body, so that the life of Jesus may also be displayed in our body. [11] For we who live are always being given over to death for Jesus's sake, so that Jesus's life may also be displayed in our mortal flesh. [12] So then, death is at work in us, but life in you. [13] And since we have the same spirit of faith in keeping with what is written, I believed, therefore I spoke, we also believe, and therefore speak. [14] For we know that the one who raised the Lord Jesus will also raise us with Jesus and present us with you. [15] Indeed, everything is for your benefit so that, as grace extends through more and more people, it may cause thanksgiving to increase to the glory of God.

[16] Therefore we do not give up. Even though our outer person is being destroyed, our inner person is being renewed day by day. [17] For our momentary light affliction is producing for us an absolutely incomparable eternal weight of glory.

[18] So we do not focus on what is seen, but on what is unseen. For what is seen is temporary, but what is unseen is eternal.

ROMANS 6:5-7

[5] For if we have been united with him in the likeness of his death, we will certainly also be in the likeness of his resurrection. [6] For we know that our old self was crucified with him so that the body ruled by sin might be rendered powerless so that we may no longer be enslaved to sin, [7] since a person who has died is freed from sin.

2 TIMOTHY 4:3

For the time will come when people will not tolerate sound doctrine, but according to their own desires, will multiply teachers for themselves because they have an itch to hear what they want to hear.

Our Future After Death

2 CORINTHIANS 5
OUR FUTURE AFTER DEATH

[1] For we know that if our earthly tent we live in is destroyed, we have a building from God, an eternal dwelling in the heavens, not made with hands. [2] Indeed, we groan in this tent, desiring to put on our heavenly dwelling, [3] since, when we have taken it off, we will not be found naked. [4] Indeed, we groan while we are in this tent, burdened as we are, because we do not want to be unclothed but clothed, so that mortality may be swallowed up by life. [5] Now the one who prepared us for this very purpose is God, who gave us the Spirit as a down payment.

[6] So we are always confident and know that while we are at home in the body we are away from the Lord. [7] For we walk by faith, not by sight. [8] In fact, we are confident, and we would prefer to be away from the body and at home with the Lord. [9] Therefore, whether we are at home or away, we make it our aim to be pleasing to him. [10] For we must all appear before the judgment seat of Christ, so that each may be repaid for what he has done in the body, whether good or evil.

[11] Therefore, since we know the fear of the Lord, we try to persuade people. What we are is plain to God, and I hope it is also plain to your consciences. [12] We are not commending ourselves to you again, but giving you an opportunity to be proud of us, so that you may have a reply for those who take pride in outward appearance rather than in the heart. [13] For if we are out of our mind, it is for God; if we are in our right mind, it is for you. [14] For the love of Christ compels us, since we have reached this conclusion: If one died for all, then all died. [15] And he died for all so that those who live should no longer live for themselves, but for the one who died for them and was raised.

THE MINISTRY OF RECONCILIATION

[16] From now on, then, we do not know anyone from a worldly perspective. Even if we have known Christ from a worldly perspective, yet now we no longer know him in this way. [17] Therefore, if anyone is in Christ, he is a new creation; the old has passed away, and see, the new has come! [18] Everything is from God, who has reconciled us

to himself through Christ and has given us the ministry of reconciliation. [19] That is, in Christ, God was reconciling the world to himself, not counting their trespasses against them, and he has committed the message of reconciliation to us.

[20] Therefore, we are ambassadors for Christ, since God is making his appeal through us. We plead on Christ's behalf: "Be reconciled to God." [21] He made the one who did not know sin to be sin for us, so that in him we might become the righteousness of God.

2 CORINTHIANS 6:1-2

[1] Working together with him, we also appeal to you, "Don't receive the grace of God in vain." [2] For he says:

At an acceptable time I listened to you,
and in the day of salvation I helped you.

See, now is the acceptable time; now is the day of salvation!

1 THESSALONIANS 4:13-18
THE COMFORT OF CHRIST'S COMING

[13] We do not want you to be uninformed, brothers and sisters, concerning those who are asleep, so that you will not grieve like the rest, who have no hope. [14] For if we believe that Jesus died and rose again, in the same way, through Jesus, God will bring with him those who have fallen asleep. [15] For we say this to you by a word from the Lord: We who are still alive at the Lord's coming will certainly not precede those who have fallen asleep. [16] For the Lord himself will descend from heaven with a shout, with the archangel's voice, and with the trumpet of God, and the dead in Christ will rise first. [17] Then we who are still alive, who are left, will be caught up together with them in the clouds to meet the Lord in the air, and so we will always be with the Lord. [18] Therefore encourage one another with these words.

TITUS 2:11-14

[11] For the grace of God has appeared, bringing salvation for all people, [12] instructing us to deny godlessness and worldly lusts and to live in a sensible, righteous, and godly way in the present age,

[13] *while we wait for the blessed hope, the appearing of the glory of our great God and Savior, Jesus Christ.*

[14] He gave himself for us to redeem us from all lawlessness and to cleanse for himself a people for his own possession, eager to do good works.

DAY 31

God's Ministers

2 CORINTHIANS 6:3-18

THE CHARACTER OF PAUL'S MINISTRY

[3] We are not giving anyone an occasion for offense, so that the ministry will not be blamed. [4] Instead, as God's ministers, we commend ourselves in everything: by great endurance, by afflictions, by hardships, by difficulties, [5] by beatings, by imprisonments, by riots, by labors, by sleepless nights, by times of hunger, [6] by purity, by knowledge, by patience, by kindness, by the Holy Spirit, by sincere love, [7] by the word of truth, by the power of God; through weapons of righteousness for the right hand and the left, [8] through glory and dishonor, through slander and good report; regarded as deceivers, yet true; [9] as unknown, yet recognized; as dying, yet see—we live; as being disciplined, yet not killed; [10] as grieving, yet always rejoicing; as poor, yet enriching many; as having nothing, yet possessing everything. [11] We have spoken openly to you, Corinthians; our heart has been opened wide. [12] We are not withholding our affection from you, but you are withholding yours from us. [13] I speak as to my children; as a proper response, open your heart to us.

SEPARATION TO GOD

[14] Don't become partners with those who do not believe. For what partnership is there between righteousness and lawlessness? Or what fellowship does light have with darkness? [15] What agreement does Christ have with Belial? Or what does a believer have in common with an unbeliever? [16] And what agreement does the temple of God have with idols? For we are the temple of the living God, as God said:

> I will dwell
> and walk among them,
> and I will be their God,
> and they will be my people.
> [17] Therefore, come out from among them
> and be separate, says the Lord;
> do not touch any unclean thing,
> and I will welcome you.
> [18] And I will be a Father to you,
> and you will be sons and daughters to me,
> says the Lord Almighty.

2 CORINTHIANS 7:1

So then, dear friends, since we have these promises, let us cleanse ourselves from every impurity of the flesh and spirit, bringing holiness to completion in the fear of God.

EZEKIEL 37:26-28

26 "I will make a covenant of peace with them; it will be a permanent covenant with them.

I will establish and multiply them and will set my sanctuary among them forever.

27 My dwelling place will be with them; I will be their God, and they will be my people. 28 When my sanctuary is among them forever, the nations will know that I, the LORD, sanctify Israel."

PHILIPPIANS 2:12-13

LIGHTS IN THE WORLD

12 Therefore, my dear friends, just as you have always obeyed, so now, not only in my presence but even more in my absence, work out your own salvation with fear and trembling. 13 For it is God who is working in you both to will and to work according to his good purpose.

What is the Church?

Throughout the New Testament, different metaphors for the community of believers are used to help us understand what the Church is and how it is meant to function.

THE FAMILY OF GOD

"...whoever does the will of my Father in heaven is my brother and sister and mother."	MT 12:49-50
...we are God's children and if children, also heirs—heirs of God and coheirs with Christ...	RM 8:16-17
"And I will be a Father to you, and you will be sons and daughters to me..."	2CO 6:18
...let us work for the good of all, especially for those who belong to the household of faith.	GL 6:10
See what great love the Father has given us that we should be called God's children—and we are!	1JN 3:1

THE BODY OF CHRIST

As it is, there are many parts, but one body.	1CO 12:20
Now you are the body of Christ, and individual members of it.	1CO 12:27
...equipping the saints for the work of ministry, to build up the body of Christ...	EPH 4:12
He is also the head of the body, the church.	COL 1:18

THE BRIDE OF CHRIST

...I have promised you in marriage to one husband—to present a pure virgin to Christ.	2CO 11:2
...just as Christ loved the church and gave himself for her to make her holy...	EPH 5:22-33
...the marriage of the Lamb has come, and his bride has prepared herself.	RV 19:7

THE LIGHT OF THE WORLD

"You are the light of the world. A city situated on a hill cannot be hidden."	MT 5:14
...the seven lampstands are the seven churches...	RV 1:20

THE PEOPLE OF GOD

| PHP 3:20 | ...but our citizenship is in heaven... |

| 1PT 2:9 | But you are a chosen race, a royal priesthood, a holy nation, a people for his possession... |

| RV 1:6 | ...and made us a kingdom, priests to his God and Father... |

| RV 21:3 | They will be his peoples, and God himself will be with them and will be their God. |

THE HOUSE OF GOD

| 1TM 3:15 | ...God's household, which is the church... |

| HEB 3:6 | Christ was faithful as a Son over his household. And we are that household... |

| EPH 2:19 | ...you are no longer foreigners and strangers, but fellow citizens with the saints, and members of God's household... |

| 1PT 2:5 | ...you yourselves, as living stones, a spiritual house, are being built to be a holy priesthood... |

THE TEMPLE OF THE SPIRIT

| 1CO 3:16-17 | ...you are God's temple and that the Spirit of God lives in you... |

| 2CO 6:16 | For we are the temple of the living God... |

| EPH 2:22 | In him you are also being built together for God's dwelling in the Spirit. |

THE FLOCK

| LK 12:32 | "Don't be afraid, little flock, because your Father delights to give you the kingdom." |

| JN 10:11 | "I am the good shepherd. The good shepherd lays down his life for the sheep." |

| AC 20:28 | Be on guard for yourselves and for all the flock of which the Holy Spirit has appointed you as overseers, to shepherd the church of God... |

| HEB 13:20 | ...our Lord Jesus—the great Shepherd of the sheep... |

CHRIST'S LETTER

| 2CO 3:3 | You show that you are Christ's letter, delivered by us, not written with ink but with the Spirit of the living God—not on tablets of stone but on tablets of human hearts. |

DAY 32

Joy and Repentance

2 CORINTHIANS 7:2-16
JOY AND REPENTANCE

2 Make room for us in your hearts. We have wronged no one, corrupted no one, taken advantage of no one. 3 I don't say this to condemn you, since I have already said that you are in our hearts, to die together and to live together. 4 I am very frank with you; I have great pride in you. I am filled with encouragement; I am overflowing with joy in all our afflictions.

5 In fact, when we came into Macedonia, we had no rest. Instead, we were troubled in every way: conflicts on the outside, fears within. 6 But God, who comforts the downcast, comforted us by the arrival of Titus, 7 and not only by his arrival but also by the comfort he received from you. He told us about your deep longing, your sorrow, and your zeal for me, so that I rejoiced even more. 8 For even if I grieved you with my letter, I don't regret it. And if I regretted it—since I saw that the letter grieved you, yet only for a while— 9 I now rejoice, not because you were grieved, but because your grief led to repentance. For you were grieved as

God willed, so that you didn't experience any loss from us. 10 For godly grief produces a repentance that leads to salvation without regret, but worldly grief produces death. 11 For consider how much diligence this very thing—this grieving as God wills—has produced in you: what a desire to clear yourselves, what indignation, what fear, what deep longing, what zeal, what justice!

In every way you showed yourselves to be pure in this matter.

12 So even though I wrote to you, it was not because of the one who did wrong, or because of the one who was wronged, but in order that your devotion to us might be made plain to you in the sight of God. 13 For this reason we have been comforted.

In addition to our own comfort, we rejoiced even more over the joy Titus had, because his spirit was refreshed by all of you. [14] For if I have made any boast to him about you, I have not been disappointed; but as I have spoken everything to you in truth, so our boasting to Titus has also turned out to be the truth. [15] And his affection toward you is even greater as he remembers the obedience of all of you, and how you received him with fear and trembling. [16] I rejoice that I have complete confidence in you.

LAMENTATIONS 3:19-24

ז *Zayin*

[19] Remember my affliction and my homelessness,
the wormwood and the poison.
[20] I continually remember them
and have become depressed.
[21] Yet I call this to mind,
and therefore I have hope:

ח *Cheth*

[22] Because of the LORD's faithful love
we do not perish,
for his mercies never end.
[23] They are new every morning;
great is your faithfulness!
[24] I say, "The LORD is my portion,
therefore I will put my hope in him."

ACTS 3:19-20

[19] Therefore repent and turn back, so that your sins may be wiped out, [20] that seasons of refreshing may come from the presence of the Lord, and that he may send Jesus, who has been appointed for you as the Messiah.

The Collection

2 CORINTHIANS 8
APPEAL TO COMPLETE THE COLLECTION

[1] We want you to know, brothers and sisters, about the grace of God that was given to the churches of Macedonia: [2] During a severe trial brought about by affliction, their abundant joy and their extreme poverty overflowed in a wealth of generosity on their part. [3] I can testify that, according to their ability and even beyond their ability, of their own accord, [4] they begged us earnestly for the privilege of sharing in the ministry to the saints, [5] and not just as we had hoped. Instead, they gave themselves first to the Lord and then to us by God's will. [6] So we urged Titus that just as he had begun, so he should also complete among you this act of grace.

[7] Now as you excel in everything—in faith, speech, knowledge, and in all diligence, and in your love for us—excel also in this act of grace. [8] I am not saying this as a command. Rather, by means of the diligence of others, I am testing the genuineness of your love. [9] For you know the grace of our Lord Jesus Christ: Though he was rich, for your sake he became poor, so that by his poverty you might become rich. [10] And in this matter I am giving advice because it is profitable for you, who began last year not only to do something but also to want to do it. [11] Now also finish the task, so that just as there was an eager desire, there may also be a completion, according to what you have. [12] For if the eagerness is there, the gift is acceptable according to what a person has, not according to what he does not have. [13] It is not that there should be relief for others and hardship for you, but it is a question of equality. [14] At the present time your surplus is available for their need, so that their abundance may in turn meet your need, in order that there may be equality. [15] As it is written: The person who had much did not have too much, and the person who had little did not have too little.

CONTINUED

FOR YOU KNOW THE GRACE
OF OUR LORD JESUS CHRIST:
THOUGH HE WAS RICH,
FOR YOUR SAKE HE BECAME POOR,
SO THAT BY HIS POVERTY YOU
MIGHT BECOME RICH.

2 CORINTHIANS 8:9

16 Thanks be to God, who put the same concern for you into the heart of Titus. 17 For he welcomed our appeal and, being very diligent, went out to you by his own choice. 18 We have sent with him the brother who is praised among all the churches for his gospel ministry. 19 And not only that, but he was also appointed by the churches to accompany us with this gracious gift that we are administering for the glory of the Lord himself and to show our eagerness to help. 20 We are taking this precaution so that no one will criticize us about this large sum that we are administering.

21 *Indeed, we are giving careful thought to do what is right, not only before the Lord but also before people.*

22 We have also sent with them our brother. We have often tested him in many circumstances and found him to be diligent—and now even more diligent because of his great confidence in you. 23 As for Titus, he is my partner and coworker for you; as for our brothers, they are the messengers of the churches, the glory of Christ. 24 Therefore, show them proof before the churches of your love and of our boasting about you.

JOHN 1:1-3

1 In the beginning was the Word, and the Word was with God, and the Word was God. 2 He was with God in the beginning. 3 All things were created through him, and apart from him not one thing was created that has been created.

PHILIPPIANS 2:4-11

4 Everyone should look out not only for his own interests, but also for the interests of others.

CHRIST'S HUMILITY AND EXALTATION

5 Adopt the same attitude as that of Christ Jesus,

6 who, existing in the form of God,
did not consider equality with God
as something to be exploited.
7 Instead he emptied himself
by assuming the form of a servant,
taking on the likeness of humanity.
And when he had come as a man,
8 he humbled himself by becoming obedient
to the point of death—
even to death on a cross.
9 For this reason God highly exalted him
and gave him the name
that is above every name,
10 so that at the name of Jesus
every knee will bow—
in heaven and on earth
and under the earth—
11 and every tongue will confess
that Jesus Christ is Lord,
to the glory of God the Father.

Crispy Pita Chips with Spinach & Artichoke Dip

INGREDIENTS: 5 | SERVES: 6

1. ROUND, STORE-BOUGHT PITA BREAD
2. OLIVE OIL
3. SALT & PEPPER
4. PARMESAN CHEESE, GRATED
5. STORE-BOUGHT SPINACH & ARTICHOKE DIP

OTHER

FOIL

DIRECTIONS

Preheat oven to 375°F. Slice each pita bread into 8 triangles and place in a large bowl. Sprinkle olive oil, salt, pepper, and parmesan cheese over pita slices and toss to coat. Arrange evenly on a foil-lined baking sheet and bake 10 minutes, turning after 5 minutes.

Spread dip evenly in a shallow casserole dish and top with fresh parmesan. Bake at 375°F for 10 to 15 minutes, until top is slightly browned.

Serve and enjoy!

GRACE DAY

Use this day to pray, rest, and reflect on this week's reading, giving thanks for the grace that is ours in Christ.

Because of the LORD's faithful love we do not perish, for his mercies never end. They are new every morning; great is your faithfulness! I say, "The LORD is my portion, therefore I will put my hope in him."

LAMENTATIONS 3:22-24

WEEKLY TRUTH

Scripture is God-breathed and true. When we memorize it, we carry the gospel with us wherever we go.

This week's verse is a summary of the gospel of Jesus.

He made the one who did not know sin to be sin for us, so that in him we might become the righteousness of God.

2 CORINTHIANS 5:21

Find the corresponding memory card in the back of this book.

"Rosa," Mixed media on canvas, 36x36

Week Six

DAY 36

Motivations for Giving

2 CORINTHIANS 9
MOTIVATIONS FOR GIVING

¹ Now concerning the ministry to the saints, it is unnecessary for me to write to you. ² For I know your eagerness, and I boast about you to the Macedonians: "Achaia has been ready since last year," and your zeal has stirred up most of them. ³ But I am sending the brothers so that our boasting about you in this matter would not prove empty, and so that you would be ready just as I said. ⁴ Otherwise, if any Macedonians come with me and find you unprepared, we, not to mention you, would be put to shame in that situation. ⁵ Therefore I considered it necessary to urge the brothers to go on ahead to you and arrange in advance the generous gift you promised, so that it will be ready as a gift and not as an extortion.

⁶ The point is this: The person who sows sparingly will also reap sparingly, and the person who sows generously will also reap generously. ⁷ Each person should do as he has decided in his heart—not reluctantly or out of compulsion, since God loves a cheerful giver. ⁸ And God is able to make every grace overflow to you, so that in every way, always having everything you need, you may excel in every good work.

[9] As it is written:

He distributed freely;
he gave to the poor;
his righteousness endures forever.

[10] Now the one who provides seed for the sower and bread for food will also provide and multiply your seed and increase the harvest of your righteousness. [11] You will be enriched in every way for all generosity, which produces thanksgiving to God through us. [12] For the ministry of this service is not only supplying the needs of the saints but is also overflowing in many expressions of thanks to God. [13] Because of the proof provided by this ministry, they will glorify God for your obedient confession of the gospel of Christ, and for your generosity in sharing with them and with everyone. [14] And as they pray on your behalf, they will have deep affection for you because of the surpassing grace of God in you. [15] Thanks be to God for his indescribable gift!

PSALM 126
ZION'S RESTORATION

A song of ascents.

[1] When the LORD restored the fortunes of Zion,
we were like those who dream.
[2] Our mouths were filled with laughter then,
and our tongues with shouts of joy.
Then they said among the nations,
"The LORD has done great things for them."
[3] The LORD had done great things for us;
we were joyful.

[4] Restore our fortunes, LORD,
like watercourses in the Negev.

[5] *Those who sow in tears will reap with shouts of joy.*

[6] Though one goes along weeping,
carrying the bag of seed,
he will surely come back with shouts of joy,
carrying his sheaves.

HOSEA 10:12
Sow righteousness for yourselves
and reap faithful love;
break up your unplowed ground.
It is time to seek the LORD
until he comes and sends righteousness
on you like the rain.

DAY 37

Paul's Apostolic Authority

2 CORINTHIANS 10
PAUL'S APOSTOLIC AUTHORITY

[1] Now I Paul, myself, appeal to you by the meekness and gentleness of Christ—I who am humble among you in person but bold toward you when absent. [2] I beg you that when I am present I will not need to be bold with the confidence by which I plan to challenge certain people who think we are behaving according to the flesh. [3] For although we live in the flesh, we do not wage war according to the flesh, [4] since the weapons of our warfare are not of the flesh, but are powerful through God for the demolition of strongholds. We demolish arguments [5] and every proud thing that is raised up against the knowledge of God, and we take every thought captive to obey Christ. [6] And we are ready to punish any disobedience, once your obedience is complete.

[7] Look at what is obvious. If anyone is confident that he belongs to Christ, let him remind himself of this: Just as he belongs to Christ, so do we. [8] For if I boast a little too much about our authority, which the Lord gave for building you up and not for tearing you down, I will not be put to shame. [9] I don't want to seem as though I am trying to terrify you with my letters. [10] For it is said, "His letters are weighty and powerful, but his physical presence is weak and his public speaking amounts to nothing." [11] Let such a person consider this: What we are in our letters, when we are absent, we will also be in our actions when we are present.

[12] For we don't dare classify or compare ourselves with some who commend themselves. But in measuring themselves by themselves and comparing themselves to themselves, they lack understanding. [13] We, however, will not boast beyond measure but according to the measure of the area of ministry that God has assigned to us, which reaches even to you. [14] For we are not overextending ourselves, as if we had not reached you, since we have come to you with the gospel of Christ. [15] We are not boasting beyond measure about other people's labors. On the contrary, we have the hope that as your faith increases, our

area of ministry will be greatly enlarged, [16] so that we may preach the gospel to the regions beyond you without boasting about what has already been done in someone else's area of ministry. [17] So let the one who boasts, boast in the Lord. [18] For it is not the one commending himself who is approved, but the one the Lord commends.

JEREMIAH 9:23-24
BOAST IN THE LORD

[23] "This is what the LORD says:

The wise person should not boast in his wisdom;
the strong should not boast in his strength;
the wealthy should not boast in his wealth.

[24] *But the one who boasts should boast in this: that he understands and knows me—*

that I am the LORD, showing faithful love,
justice, and righteousness on the earth,
for I delight in these things.
This is the LORD's declaration."

EPHESIANS 2:8-9

[8] For you are saved by grace through faith, and this is not from yourselves; it is God's gift— [9] not from works, so that no one can boast.

Paul's Sufferings for Christ

2 CORINTHIANS 11
PAUL AND THE FALSE APOSTLES

[1] I wish you would put up with a little foolishness from me. Yes, do put up with me! [2] For I am jealous for you with a godly jealousy, because I have promised you in marriage to one husband—to present a pure virgin to Christ. [3] But I fear that, as the serpent deceived Eve by his cunning, your minds may be seduced from a sincere and pure devotion to Christ. [4] For if a person comes and preaches another Jesus, whom we did not preach, or you receive a different spirit, which you had not received, or a different gospel, which you had not accepted, you put up with it splendidly!

[5] Now I consider myself in no way inferior to those "super-apostles." [6] Even if I am untrained in public speaking, I am certainly not untrained in knowledge. Indeed, we have in every way made that clear to you in everything. [7] Or did I commit a sin by humbling myself so that you might be exalted, because I preached the gospel of God to you free of charge? [8] I robbed other churches by taking pay from them to minister to you.

> [9] *When I was present with you and in need, I did not burden anyone,*

since the brothers who came from Macedonia supplied my needs. I have kept myself, and will keep myself, from burdening you in any way. [10] As the truth of Christ is in me, this boasting of mine will not be stopped in the regions of Achaia. [11] Why? Because I don't love you? God knows I do!

[12] But I will continue to do what I am doing, in order to deny an opportunity to those who want to be regarded as our equals in what they boast about. [13] For such people are false apostles, deceitful workers, disguising themselves as apostles of Christ. [14] And no wonder! For Satan disguises himself as an angel of light. [15] So it is no great surprise if his servants also disguise themselves as servants of righteousness. Their end will be according to their works.

PAUL'S SUFFERINGS FOR CHRIST

¹⁶ I repeat: Let no one consider me a fool. But if you do, at least accept me as a fool so that I can also boast a little. ¹⁷ What I am saying in this matter of boasting, I don't speak as the Lord would, but as it were, foolishly. ¹⁸ Since many boast according to the flesh, I will also boast. ¹⁹ For you, being so wise, gladly put up with fools! ²⁰ In fact, you put up with it if someone enslaves you, if someone exploits you, if someone takes advantage of you, if someone is arrogant toward you, if someone slaps you in the face. ²¹ I say this to our shame: We have been too weak for that!

But in whatever anyone dares to boast—I am talking foolishly—I also dare: ²² Are they Hebrews? So am I. Are they Israelites? So am I. Are they the descendants of Abraham? So am I. ²³ Are they servants of Christ? I'm talking like a madman—I'm a better one: with far more labors, many more imprisonments, far worse beatings, many times near death.

²⁴ Five times I received the forty lashes minus one from the Jews. ²⁵ Three times I was beaten with rods. Once I received a stoning. Three times I was shipwrecked. I have spent a night and a day in the open sea. ²⁶ On frequent journeys, I faced dangers from rivers, dangers from robbers, dangers from my own people, dangers from Gentiles, dangers in the city, dangers in the wilderness, dangers at sea, and dangers among false brothers; ²⁷ toil and hardship, many sleepless nights, hunger and thirst, often without food, cold, and without clothing. ²⁸ Not to mention other things, there is the daily pressure on me: my concern for all the churches. ²⁹ Who is weak, and I am not weak? Who is made to stumble, and I do not burn with indignation?

³⁰ If boasting is necessary, I will boast about my weaknesses. ³¹ The God and Father of the Lord Jesus, who is blessed forever, knows I am not lying. ³² In Damascus, a ruler under King Aretas guarded the city of Damascus in order to arrest me. ³³ So I was let down in a basket through a window in the wall and escaped from his hands.

JOHN 3:29

He who has the bride is the groom. But the groom's friend, who stands by and listens for him, rejoices greatly at the groom's voice. So this joy of mine is complete.

REVELATION 19:7-8

⁷ Let us be glad, rejoice, and give him glory,
because the marriage of the Lamb has come,
and his bride has prepared herself.
⁸ She was given fine linen to wear, bright and pure.

For the fine linen represents the righteous acts of the saints.

DAY 39

Sufficient Grace

2 CORINTHIANS 12

SUFFICIENT GRACE

STUDY QUESTIONS ON P. 164

¹ Boasting is necessary. It is not profitable, but I will move on to visions and revelations of the Lord. ² I know a man in Christ who was caught up to the third heaven fourteen years ago. Whether he was in the body or out of the body, I don't know; God knows. ³ I know that this man—whether in the body or out of the body I don't know; God knows— ⁴ was caught up into paradise and heard inexpressible words, which a human being is not allowed to speak. ⁵ I will boast about this person, but not about myself, except of my weaknesses.

⁶ For if I want to boast, I wouldn't be a fool, because I would be telling the truth. But I will spare you, so that no one can credit me with something beyond what he sees in me or hears from me, ⁷ especially because of the extraordinary revelations. Therefore, so that I would not exalt myself, a thorn in the flesh was given to me, a messenger of Satan to torment me so that I would not exalt myself. ⁸ Concerning this, I pleaded with the Lord three times that it would leave me. ⁹ But he said to me, "My grace is sufficient for you, for my power is perfected in weakness."

Therefore, I will most gladly boast all the more about my weaknesses, so that Christ's power may reside in me. ¹⁰ So I take pleasure in weaknesses, insults, hardships, persecutions, and in difficulties, for the sake of Christ. For when I am weak, then I am strong.

SIGNS OF AN APOSTLE

¹¹ I have been a fool; you forced it on me. You ought to have commended me, since I am not in any way inferior to those "super-apostles," even though I am nothing. ¹² The signs of an apostle were performed with unfailing endurance among you, including signs and wonders and miracles. ¹³ So in what way are you worse off than the other churches, except that I personally did not burden you? Forgive me for this wrong!

CONTINUED

BUT HE SAID TO ME,
"MY GRACE IS SUFFICIENT FOR YOU,
FOR MY POWER IS
PERFECTED IN WEAKNESS."

2 CORINTHIANS 12:9

[14] Look, I am ready to come to you this third time. I will not burden you, since I am not seeking what is yours, but you. For children ought not save up for their parents, but parents for their children. [15] I will most gladly spend and be spent for you. If I love you more, am I to be loved less? [16] Now granted, I did not burden you; yet sly as I am, I took you in by deceit! [17] Did I take advantage of you by any of those I sent you? [18] I urged Titus to go, and I sent the brother with him. Titus didn't take advantage of you, did he? Didn't we walk in the same spirit and in the same footsteps?

[19] Have you been thinking all along that we were defending ourselves to you? No, in the sight of God we are speaking in Christ, and everything, dear friends, is for building you up. [20] For I fear that perhaps when I come I will not find you to be what I want, and you may not find me to be what you want. Perhaps there will be quarreling, jealousy, angry outbursts, selfish ambitions, slander, gossip, arrogance, and disorder. [21] I fear that when I come my God will again humiliate me in your presence, and I will grieve for many who sinned before and have not repented of the moral impurity, sexual immorality, and sensuality they practiced.

MARK 14:32-36
THE PRAYER IN THE GARDEN

[32] Then they came to a place named Gethsemane, and he told his disciples, "Sit here while I pray." [33] He took Peter, James, and John with him, and he began to be deeply distressed and troubled. [34] He said to them, "I am deeply grieved to the point of death. Remain here and stay awake." [35] He went a little farther, fell to the ground, and prayed that if it were possible, the hour might pass from him. [36] And he said, "Abba, Father! All things are possible for you. Take this cup away from me. Nevertheless, not what I will, but what you will."

PHILIPPIANS 4:10-13
APPRECIATION OF SUPPORT

[10] I rejoiced in the Lord greatly because once again you renewed your care for me. You were, in fact, concerned about me but lacked the opportunity to show it. [11] I don't say this out of need, for I have learned to be content in whatever circumstances I find myself. [12] I know both how to make do with little, and I know how to make do with a lot. In any and all circumstances I have learned the secret of being content—whether well fed or hungry, whether in abundance or in need. [13] I am able to do all things through him who strengthens me.

DAY 40

Finally, Rejoice

2 CORINTHIANS 13
FINAL WARNINGS AND EXHORTATIONS

¹ This is the third time I am coming to you. Every matter must be established by the testimony of two or three witnesses. ² I gave a warning when I was present the second time, and now I give a warning while I am absent to those who sinned before and to all the rest: If I come again, I will not be lenient, ³ since you seek proof of Christ speaking in me. He is not weak in dealing with you, but powerful among you. ⁴ For he was crucified in weakness, but he lives by the power of God. For we also are weak in him, but in dealing with you we will live with him by God's power.

⁵ Test yourselves to see if you are in the faith. Examine yourselves. Or do you yourselves not recognize that Jesus Christ is in you?—unless you fail the test. ⁶ And I hope you will recognize that we ourselves do not fail the test. ⁷ But we pray to God that you do nothing wrong—not that we may appear to pass the test, but that you may do what is right, even though we may appear to fail.

> ⁸ _For we can't do anything against the truth, but only for the truth._

⁹ We rejoice when we are weak and you are strong. We also pray that you become fully mature. ¹⁰ This is why I am writing these things while absent, so that when I am there I may not have to deal harshly with you, in keeping with the authority the Lord gave me for building up and not for tearing down.

¹¹ Finally, brothers and sisters, rejoice. Become mature, be encouraged, be of the same mind, be at peace, and the God of love and peace will be with you. ¹² Greet one another with a holy kiss. All the saints send you greetings.

¹³ The grace of the Lord Jesus Christ, and the love of God, and the fellowship of the Holy Spirit be with you all.

JOHN 15:1-8
THE VINE AND THE BRANCHES

[1] "I am the true vine, and my Father is the gardener. [2] Every branch in me that does not produce fruit he removes, and he prunes every branch that produces fruit so that it will produce more fruit. [3] You are already clean because of the word I have spoken to you. [4] Remain in me, and I in you. Just as a branch is unable to produce fruit by itself unless it remains on the vine, neither can you unless you remain in me. [5] I am the vine; you are the branches. The one who remains in me and I in him produces much fruit, because you can do nothing without me. [6] If anyone does not remain in me, he is thrown aside like a branch and he withers. They gather them, throw them into the fire, and they are burned. [7] If you remain in me and my words remain in you, ask whatever you want and it will be done for you. [8] My Father is glorified by this: that you produce much fruit and prove to be my disciples."

COLOSSIANS 1:9-12
PRAYER FOR SPIRITUAL GROWTH

[9] For this reason also, since the day we heard this, we haven't stopped praying for you. We are asking that you may be filled with the knowledge of his will in all wisdom and spiritual understanding, [10] so that you may walk worthy of the Lord, fully pleasing to him: bearing fruit in every good work and growing in the knowledge of God, [11] being strengthened with all power, according to his glorious might, so that you may have great endurance and patience, joyfully [12] giving thanks to the Father, who has enabled you to share in the saints' inheritance in the light.

Chocolate Twist Bread

INGREDIENTS: 3 | MAKES: 1 BREAD TWIST

1

1 CAN CRESCENT
ROLL DOUGH

2

¼ CUP HAZELNUT OR
CHOCOLATE SPREAD

3

POWDERED SUGAR

OTHER

FOIL

PARCHMENT PAPER

DIRECTIONS

Preheat oven to 375°F.

Unroll dough onto a clean surface. Seal perforated edges by gently pinching dough together. Evenly coat with the spread, edge to edge.

Position dough lengthwise in front of you and tightly roll the dough away from you.

Place on a baking sheet lined with parchment paper. Leaving ½ inch at one end, use a sharp knife to divide the entire roll lengthwise down the middle.

Gently rotate each half away from the center so the layered inside is facing up. Bring one half over the other. Repeat. Continue to twist, inside facing up, until you reach the end, then pinch the two ends to seal them together.

Cover loosely with foil and bake 17 to 20 minutes, removing foil halfway through. Let bread cool, and dust with powdered sugar before serving.

SERVE WITH WARM HAZELNUT
SPREAD IN BOWLS FOR DIPPING

GRACE DAY

Use this day to pray, rest, and reflect on this week's reading, giving thanks for the grace that is ours in Christ.

Sow righteousness for yourselves
and reap faithful love;
break up your unplowed ground.
It is time to seek the LORD
until he comes and sends righteousness
on you like the rain.

HOSEA 10:12

WEEKLY TRUTH

Scripture is God-breathed and true. When we memorize it, we carry the gospel with us wherever we go.

This week we will memorize the key verse for 2 Corinthians.

But he said to me, "My grace is sufficient for you, for my power is perfected in weakness." Therefore, I will most gladly boast all the more about my weaknesses, so that Christ's power may reside in me.

2 CORINTHIANS 12:9

Find the corresponding memory card in the back of this book.

WEEKS 1–6

Study Questions

Use this section for personal study, or gather some friends and neighbors, make a recipe or two from this book, and discuss these questions. Each set of questions includes notes from the CSB Study Bible.

WEEK 1: *Christ the Power and Wisdom of God*

1 CORINTHIANS 1:18-25

[18] For the word of the cross is foolishness to those who are perishing, but it is the power of God to us who are being saved. [19] For it is written,

> I will destroy the wisdom of the wise,
> and I will set aside the intelligence of the intelligent.

[20] Where is the one who is wise? Where is the teacher of the law? Where is the debater of this age? Hasn't God made the world's wisdom foolish? [21] For since, in God's wisdom, the world did not know God through wisdom, God was pleased to save those who believe through the foolishness of what is preached. [22] For the Jews ask for signs and the Greeks seek wisdom, [23] but we preach Christ crucified, a stumbling block to the Jews and foolishness to the Gentiles. [24] Yet to those who are called, both Jews and Greeks, Christ is the power of God and the wisdom of God, [25] because God's foolishness is wiser than human wisdom, and God's weakness is stronger than human strength.

1 Why do you think people would have regarded the "word of the cross" of Jesus as foolishness?

2 How would you describe the "world's wisdom" and "God's wisdom"? How are they different? What does worldly wisdom value? What does godly wisdom value?

3 In what ways is the cross "the power of God to us who are being saved"?

WEEK 2: *Glorifying God in Body and Spirit*

CSB STUDY NOTES

6:12

Paul quotes a slogan apparently put forth by the immature Corinthians, "Everything is permissible for me," to introduce a series of admonitions emphasizing...a believer's freedom is to be limited to that which is profitable to the Lord.

6:15-17

"One flesh" recalls Genesis 2:24 and contrasts the proper mariage relationship with an illicit sexual relationship.

6:18-20

The believer's body is a sacred vessel, "bought at a price" by the Son of God. Believers thus have no business doing anything with the Lord's body that does not glorify Him.

1 CORINTHIANS 6:12-20

[12] "Everything is permissible for me," but not everything is beneficial. "Everything is permissible for me," but I will not be mastered by anything. [13] "Food is for the stomach and the stomach for food," and God will do away with both of them. However, the body is not for sexual immorality but for the Lord, and the Lord for the body. [14] God raised up the Lord and will also raise us up by his power. [15] Don't you know that your bodies are a part of Christ's body? So should I take a part of Christ's body and make it part of a prostitute? Absolutely not! [16] Don't you know that anyone joined to a prostitute is one body with her? For Scripture says, The two will become one flesh. [17] But anyone joined to the Lord is one spirit with him.

[18] Flee sexual immorality! Every other sin a person commits is outside the body, but the person who is sexually immoral sins against his own body. [19] Don't you know that your body is a temple of the Holy Spirit who is in you, whom you have from God? You are not your own, [20] for you were bought at a price. So glorify God with your body.

1 What are some things that are permissible, but are not beneficial? What is the wisdom in the statement, "Everything is permissible for me, but not everything is beneficial"?

2 What does it mean to say that a Christian's body is a "temple of the Holy Spirit who is in you, whom you have from God"? What does it mean that we are not our own?

3 Does it surprise you that the Bible talks about the value of our physical bodies? Why or why not? How would you summarize what these verses say about how God views the human body?

WEEK 3: *Unity and Diversity in the Body*

CSB STUDY NOTES

2 CORINTHIANS 12:1-10

12:13

Through the work of "one Spirit," individual believers become identified as "one body" of Christ. "All" believers are "baptized" into one body and are "given one Spirit to drink."

12:18

The dispersion and diversification of gifts is no accident. God Himself has given them "just as he wanted."

12:23-26

God has arranged the body of Christ in such a way that the "less honorable" members are accorded "greater honor." Humility is a pinnacle value in the kingdom of God.

[12] For just as the body is one and has many parts, and all the parts of that body, though many, are one body—so also is Christ. [13] For we were all baptized by one Spirit into one body—whether Jews or Greeks, whether slaves or free—and we were all given one Spirit to drink. [14] Indeed, the body is not one part but many. [15] If the foot should say, "Because I'm not a hand, I don't belong to the body," it is not for that reason any less a part of the body. [16] And if the ear should say, "Because I'm not an eye, I don't belong to the body," it is not for that reason any less a part of the body. [17] If the whole body were an eye, where would the hearing be? If the whole body were an ear, where would the sense of smell be? [18] But as it is, God has arranged each one of the parts in the body just as he wanted. [19] And if they were all the same part, where would the body be? [20] As it is, there are many parts, but one body. [21] The eye cannot say to the hand, "I don't need you!" Or again, the head can't say to the feet, "I don't need you!" [22] On the contrary, those parts of the body that are weaker are indispensable. [23] And those parts of the body that we consider less honorable, we clothe these with greater honor, and our unrespectable parts are treated with greater respect, [24] which our respectable parts do not need.

Instead, God has put the body together, giving greater honor to the less honorable, [25] so that there would be no division in the body, but that the members would have the same concern for each other. [26] So if one member suffers, all the members suffer with it; if one member is honored, all the members rejoice with it.

1 Are there certain gifts you wish you had? What about them makes you wish they were yours?

2 What gifts do you have that are of value to the body of Christ as a whole, and how do you use them? If you struggle to use your gifts, what do you think would help?

3 What do you think verses 22–26, which talk about "weak" and "less honorable" parts, are saying? What do these verses teach us about humility?

WEEK 4: *Victorious Resurrection*

1 CORINTHIANS 15:50-58

15:51-52

Though not every-one will die ("fall asleep") before Christ's coming, those who are alive when He comes "will all be changed." No one is transported to the eternal state unchanged.

15:52

"Twinkling of an eye" implies rapidity. Such will be the swiftness of the transformation of the living when "the last trumpet" sounds at Christ's return.

15:57

Christ brings not only victory over death in the res-urrection but also victory over sin that leads to death.

⁵⁰ What I am saying, brothers and sisters, is this: Flesh and blood cannot inherit the kingdom of God, nor can corruption inherit incorruption. ⁵¹ Listen, I am telling you a mystery: We will not all fall asleep, but we will all be changed, ⁵² in a moment, in the twinkling of an eye, at the last trumpet. For the trumpet will sound, and the dead will be raised incorruptible, and we will be changed. ⁵³ For this corruptible body must be clothed with incorruptibility, and this mortal body must be clothed with immortality. ⁵⁴ When this corruptible body is clothed with incorruptibility, and this mortal body is clothed with immortality, then the saying that is written will take place:

Death has been swallowed up in victory.
⁵⁵ Where, death, is your victory?
Where, death, is your sting?

⁵⁶ The sting of death is sin, and the power of sin is the law. ⁵⁷ But thanks be to God, who gives us the victory through our Lord Jesus Christ!

⁵⁸ Therefore, my dear brothers and sisters, be steadfast, immovable, always excelling in the Lord's work, because you know that your labor in the Lord is not in vain.

1 1 Corinthians 15 focuses on the resurrection of Christ and believers. Is there anything in this passage that surprises you? Confuses you? Encourages you?

2 According to these verses, what is the "sting of death" and how are we given victory over it? How has death been "swallowed up in victory"?

3 Since death has been defeated, what does Paul say should be our response? Why? How is this response difficult or easy for you?

WEEK 5: *Treasure in Clay Jars*

CSB STUDY NOTES

2 CORINTHIANS 4:7-18

4:7

"Clay jars" is a metaphor for fragile and mortal human bodies. Sometimes the more humble the container, the more glorious and precious its contents appear.

4:10-11

In His humanity Jesus was subject to death; by God's power He was raised to resurrection life. Paul (and indeed all the saints) would follow Jesus' example.

4:14

The words "us with you" show that the resurrection of the saints is not individualistic... [It] emphasizes the corporate nature of the Church.

[7] Now we have this treasure in clay jars, so that this extraordinary power may be from God and not from us. [8] We are afflicted in every way but not crushed; we are perplexed but not in despair; [9] we are persecuted but not abandoned; we are struck down but not destroyed. [10] We always carry the death of Jesus in our body, so that the life of Jesus may also be displayed in our body. [11] For we who live are always being given over to death for Jesus's sake, so that Jesus's life may also be displayed in our mortal flesh. [12] So then, death is at work in us, but life in you. [13] And since we have the same spirit of faith in keeping with what is written, I believed, therefore I spoke, we also believe, and therefore speak. [14] For we know that the one who raised the Lord Jesus will also raise us with Jesus and present us with you. [15] Indeed, everything is for your benefit so that, as grace extends through more and more people, it may cause thanksgiving to increase to the glory of God.

[16] Therefore we do not give up. Even though our outer person is being destroyed, our inner person is being renewed day by day. [17] For our momentary light affliction is producing for us an absolutely incomparable eternal weight of glory. [18] So we do not focus on what is seen, but on what is unseen. For what is seen is temporary, but what is unseen is eternal.